The Borough of Enfield
Memories

*The publishers would like to thank the following companies for their
support in the production of this book*

Main Sponsor
Enfield Timber Company

G Farley

First National Retail Finance

GE Lighting

Johnson Matthey

LondonWaste Limited

Long & Somerville (Enfield) Limited

Merck Sharp & Company

Morelli & Company

Centre Management, Palace Gardens Shopping Centre

Pearsons (Enfield) Limited

Rayner & Company Limited

RA Haulage

Turnomatic Limited

GR Wright & Sons

Yoplait Dairy Crest

First published in Great Britain by True North Books
England HX5 9AE
Telephone: 01422 377977
© **True North Books Limited 2000**

ISBN 1 903204 14 3

*Text, design and origination by True North Books Limited
Printed and bound by The Amadeus Press Limited*

The Borough of
Enfield
Memories

Edited by Stephen Sellick

Contents

Introduction

W e have all taken to the road on our travels. Many of us have taken to the air. Others use the seas around our island. But with 'Memories of Enfield' it is an opportunity to indulge in time travel. There is no magical Tardis to transport you back through history. What we have is page after page of nostalgia. Wonderful images, all carefully captioned with informative and witty text, will help the reader return to the last century without ever leaving the armchair in which he is sitting.

As you turn each leaf you will be able to share those days when dad was a lad or grandma was a flapper. Our towns and boroughs have changed so much since their times that it is hard to bring to mind just how everything used to be. Thank goodness for the camera. Without a pictorial record so much of our recent history would be a mere memory. You know how unreliable memories are. The mind can play tricks, but the camera never lies. All the pictures and photographs are accompanied by words that sharpen the recollections you might have. You will have personal experience of some of the scenes. Others will be brought to mind by the stories our parents and grandparents told us. In this book you will be

able to see what it was they were talking about when referring to certain streets and events. There are other photographs and memory joggers that you will be able to remember for yourself. Perhaps this book might even settle a wager or two. Quite often people remember the same occasion or place in different ways. If there is a fact or picture in this book that helps you win the bet, then good luck. However if it was your memory that was playing tricks, then you can always turn to the next page! There will be plenty more of interest to follow.

'Memories of Enfield' is not intended to be a dry and dusty old history book. It is meant to be a means for the reader to indulge in a wave of nostalgia for a century that is not too far behind us, but is growing more distant with each passing day. The 20th century brought us so much. The aeroplane flew for the first time. Electrical appliances changed the way we ran our households and entertained ourselves. Women were liberated and the country became a multicultural society. Villages grew into towns and industry replaced agriculture as our setting. New and ever wider roads swept away the lanes and cottages of our heritage. Little shops became supermarkets. Tower blocks rose on the skyline. The computer chip replaced the brain. Without pictorial records of the past we would only be able

to rely on the written or spoken word for our nostalgia. But, with 'Memories of Enfield', there is a chance to claw back those days of yesteryear. Sit your children down and leaf through the book with them. They are our future, but they must not be allowed to ignore their heritage. Make sure that they have cameras of their own so that they can repeat the process for generations to come. They must learn from our mistakes and build on our successes. Nostalgia does not mean that you are wallowing in the past. You are just remembering the good times and shedding a silent tear when it less than so. Not everything in your background is wonderful, but it would be a crime to be unable to preserve those bits that were.

The borough of Enfield is a cosmopolitan area. Included in it are the major centres of Edmonton and Southgate. Sometimes these places tend to regard themselves as separate identities, under one banner heading as they are. 'Memories of Enfield' tries to balance the flavour of separate communities within the borough as a whole. Smaller areas, such as Ponders End, Palmers Green,

Winchmore Hill and Bush Hill Park, also have a part to play. Although the Romans had settlements in the district, Enfield Town can trace its true origins to Anglo Saxon times. Its name means 'a field belonging to Eana' and was mentioned in the 1086 Domesday Book. This famous work refers to a priest living there. It must have been close to the site of the present parish church of St Andrew's. There was a manor house, later nicknamed 'The Palace', that was to become the place where Enfield now shops, the Palace Gardens Shopping Precinct. Until the 19th century the area was a collection of hamlets, only loosely connected with one another. The present borough of Enfield was largely rural and parts of the district were heavily wooded. The Arnos and Grovelands estates were covered with magnificent oaks. Royalty hunted in the fields and forests. Farms dotted the landscape. Cattle grazed and crops were grown in a sleepy and peaceful country atmosphere.

The age of the railway changed so much. All of a sudden London became easily accessible. The first true commuters came to live here. A population of just over 11,000 in 1801

doubled in 50 years. Although the real industrial revolution took place near the more northern coalfields and iron ore sites, Enfield had its share of the new smoky age. A crepe mill, the Royal Small Arms Factory, a gas works, a jute mill and linoleum factories had all appeared by the mid 19th century. However, the main development came at the turn of the century when electricity came to the town both as an amenity and as an industry.

At the beginning of the 20th century Enfield was still largely rural. It was the housing developments after World War I that began to change this. Market gardens and orchards gave way to housing estates. Even so, it was not until about the time of the start of the second world war that the rural gap between here and outer London disappeared. Southgate and Edmonton became boroughs in the 1930s, but Enfield did not achieve the same status until 1955. Ten years later they combined as the London Borough of Enfield. Pour a shot of Tizer, suck on a gobstopper and put on a record (remember them?) of someone who was popular before even Cliff Richard was heard of. It is time to go on that journey back through time. Dressed in hot pants from the 1970s or cloche hats from the 1920s, return to the days when Biggles ruled the skies and Alf Tupper ran on the track faster than any Olympian. Do not be afraid to speak out loud, 'Well, I had forgotten that was there.' When you read 'Memories of Enfield' so much will come back to surprise and thrill you. Return to days when little girls wore white socks and men stood up on the Tube to let a lady have a seat. Relive the times when shopkeepers wiped their hands on their aprons and asked after your family. See once more the pubs where we could relax without having our ears blasted by hiphop music. But, best of all, drift off into a world of your own, brought back to you courtesy of this delightful book. Open your packet of Spangles and switch off that mobile phone. Turning the very first page launches the nostalgia trip. Do not let anything disturb those cherished memories. For some of us Max Bygraves once sang it out clearly with 'Fings ain't what they used to be'.

Street scenes

Above: This idyllic scene dates from 1922. It was a time of getting back into our stride after the horrors of The Great War. Life would never be the same again for families who had left so many of their young men in the mud of the trenches at Flanders, Ypres and the Somme. Some of the physical scars were healing, but the mental ones remained. The shops in St Mark's Road have changed the type of goods they sell and the frontages now look different. But, apart from that, this road still has a similar look in the 21st century. Bush Hill Park Hotel, at the top of the picture, has stood there since 1896. Whitbread built the grand edifice so that it stood out above its neighbours. Various alterations in 1948, 1962 and 1993

have now made the interior a more open space, replacing the original smaller rooms. Just out of shot, to the right of the hotel, is the station that opened in 1880. There was a great deal of concern about pubs like the Bush Hill when it first opened. Drunkenness was the scourge of some family life. By 1914 there were 1,287 prosecutions per week. Not all these were linked with the Bush Hill Park Hotel, it must be said! About the only virtue of the war was the reduction it brought to those figures. Higher tax, shorter opening hours and a 'no treating' order brought the number of court cases down to 263 in a week by 1917. The no treating measure meant that you had to buy your own drink or risk a 10 shilling fine.

There were few cars around The Town in the late 1920s. The tram going towards Church Street has the scene almost to itself. It would have stopped by Barclays Bank on the right, with the site where Pearson's store would be open after redevelopment in 1931 on the left. The fountain, with its two delightful cherubs, still stands proudly where London Road and Silver Street join The Town. It was erected in 1884, thanks to public subscription. When Enfield Council arranged for its restoration in 1994 townspeople were again asked to contribute to the cost. Customers of Marks and Spencer provided the donations. A plaque on the fountain states that the Rotary Club of Enfield, in memory of Henry Joshua Brown (1906-83), sponsored it. He was a past president of the Rotary Club and a well known local horticulturist. The overhead cables of the tram system have long gone. Perhaps the tracks might return one day in the future, but it is unlikely. Some larger cities have begun to reintroduce them or consider doing so. Manchester, Sheffield, Newcastle and Leeds are amongst those that have turned the clock back or thought about doing so. But they have more space than Enfield. It is hard to imagine that our crowded streets and bumper to bumper traffic around the one way system could accommodate the return of the tram. But, something has to happen. The 21st century could bring us a complete ban on the motor car in town centres. The way things are going something has to give before we end up completely gridlocked.

Above: Much of the architecture on Church Street in the 1930s dated from the beginning of the century. The middle section on the left, just beyond the optician's, was built in 1916. This was unusual. Not many major building projects were undertaken in wartime. Materials and energies were usually directed towards defeating the enemy. The buildings on either side date from 1908. Burleigh House used to stand near here, behind on the left. It was vacated in 1912 and demolished the following year. The Rialto Cinema, later a bingo hall, attracted customers to the edge of Burleigh Way. Errol Flynn in 'The Charge of the Light Brigade', Ronald Colman in 'A Tale of Two Cities', Merle Oberon in 'The Scarlet Pimpernel' and Anna Neagle in 'As You Like It' were all box office hits of the decade. Packed audiences were wowed by those early talkies. A night at the pictures was a regular weekly treat. Sweethearts cuddled on the back row until usherettes shone their torches on them. Hollywood stars became household names. On their way home couples discussed the smouldering good looks of Leslie Howard or fantasised about the charms of Mary Pickford.

Above right: In 1931 the photographer sat on top of Southgate Station to catch this shot. The development of this area was not completed until 1933. By then the Tube had reached Southgate and the roundabout and traffic islands in place. A new block of shops, Dennis Parade, replaced the advertisers' posters on the far side of the Circus. The lorry entering the picture came from Chase Side. It was probably headed off past the hoardings and up Winchmore Hill Road. The Bell, on the corner of Chase Road, was one of the town's oldest pubs. For years its taproom had echoed to the clack of dominoes. Games of fives and threes, pegged on a crib board, were hard fought contests between friends who regularly met there. Youngsters brought up on a 21st century diet of PlayStations and computer games may have no idea of what a crib board looks like. The modern generation has missed out on the world of cribbage. The card game was very popular and had a language of its own. 'Morgan's orchard', 'one for his nob' and 'Harry Tate' are terms understood by lovers of the game. To the nerd they are gibberish. Some pubs still take part in a crib league, but they are on the decline. Players in the Bell had to go somewhere else after 1963. There was further development of this corner and the pub was demolished. The barber next door also shaved his last customer and took down his striped pole.

Right: We are back in 1925. Pots and pans cluttered the pavement outside the stores. The strong aroma of Balkan Sobranie mixture and thick twist wafted out from the tobacconist's. Even non smokers enjoyed the subtle smells that drifted through the door. Inside there was a grand choice of briars, meerschaums and clay pipes. Imported Turkish cigarettes were a luxury item for high days and holidays. In the centre of the street a horse and cart slowly wheeled a milk churn across The Town towards the Nag's Head. Its pointed roof turret was remarkably similar to that on the King's Head at Winchmore Hill. This was the second Nag's Head on this site. It was built in 1883. Rebuilding took place once more in 1932 when Southbury Road was widened. The pub closed in the early 1960s. Wendy's Boutique took over the ground floor. That was a typical shop of the swinging 60s. Boutiques, aping the success of Carnaby Street, were all the rage with the baby boomers, born in the late 40s and with money to spend in young adulthood. They thought they belonged to the first generation to take an interest in trendy fashion for young people. The generation of 1925 beat them to it. After World War I liberated young women started applying make up and wearing it in public. They cropped their hair short. Cloche hats neatly fitted over the new style and they wore flapper dresses to dance the Charleston.

Below: The bus stop on the right and the light on the trolley bus cabling disappeared in 1961. The cars heading towards the camera from the direction of the old Nag's Head date from the early 1950s. On the left, the London and Provincial Bank had once owned the building occupied by Barclays Bank. It opened after the 1897 demolition of the public offices and courthouse that once stood here. Before those times the Greyhound Inn, a large brick building, was on this site. Its Dutch gables had stood there since the 17th century. The pub lost its licence to sell liquor in 1860 and the whole nature of the place changed dramatically. This branch of Barclays holds a unique place in the history of British banking. In June 1967 it was the first to have an automatic cash dispenser. Some people actually believed it was the bank showing its more kindly side. They thought that it was a way of redistributing its profits to the customer. They had an awful shock when they checked their bank statements at the end of the month. Banking has undergone a revolution in the last few years. Building societies have demutualised. Hole in the wall dispensers give us access to our money at all hours of the day and night. We can transfer funds at the press of a phone button or move money about via the internet. Going up to the counter to speak to a bank teller will soon be a thing of the past.

Left: The building in the distance, next to the parked van, belonged to Tottenham and Edmonton Gas. It was only there during 1914-37. Across the road from Burleigh Way, the mighty jeweller's clock hung above the street. It meant that there was no need to go into the shop to buy a watch. The time could clearly be seen the length of Church Street in the early 1930s. In the Lilley and Skinner shop next door, assistants fitted shoes to the daintiest of feet. The company, particularly popular across the south of England, traded here for most of the 20th century. The doors only closed in about 1980. Over the way Saville's Pianos kept its name as a link to former times. Most middle class families had a 'joanna' in the house, though it was infra dig to call it such a common name. As tastes changed, the instrumental side of the business played 'second fiddle' to its growing importance as a record store. It has now been owned by HMV for some 20 years. Nipper, the dog on the company logo, now looks out across Church Street. Once the public bought gramophone records that played on wind up machines. Needles had to be changed after every play. They hissed and crackled out tunes that became standards in time. Delivery boys whistled ''On the Sunny Side of the Street', 'Just One More Chance' and 'Stormy Weather'. Imagine trying to hum 'Freak Me' or 'Snoop's Upside Ya Head' these days. Imagine even wanting to.

Below: In 1958 the second bus was advertising Bisto. The sight of those Bisto kids sniffing the juicy gravy aroma was enough to set your mouth watering. Roast beef of old England is never quite the same without a jugful of Bisto to accompany it. We are looking at a time when at last we could afford to eat well. The austere postwar years and the restrictions of rationing were behind us. Britain was booming and the government was keen to tell us so. Prime Minister Harold Macmillan won the following year's general election on the slogan, 'You've never had it so good.' It was a period of near full employment and the nation was ready to throw off the shackles of shortages. We had money in our pockets and the shops were bursting with goods to tempt us. Washing machines, fridges, televisions and motor cars became standard possessions. They were luxury items to our parents, but we came to regard them as necessities. A new consumer group was recognised. The teenager had a share of the market. Clothes were specially styled for them. They also demanded their own style of entertainment. They went to a coffee bar rather than Lyons' tea rooms. Jimmy Young and Dickie Valentine were out. Buddy Holly and Eddie Cochran were in. Both these teen idols became permanently fixed in the youth culture of the day when they died at the height of their fame. Buddy was killed in a plane crash in 1959 and Eddie in a car smash the following year.

By the mid 1960s all trace of the trolley buses had disappeared from our streets. Looking east towards the London Road junction on the right, the traffic flowed both ways until the start of the next decade. The one way system that was introduced did its best to keep traffic on the move. British cars still dominated the scene.

The well to do had the Jaguar and the flashy set ran an Austin Healey sports car. More humble souls made do with a Mini. The land of the rising sun had yet to make its mark. We drove around in cars called Elf, Imp, Victor, Cowley and Oxford. The days of weird and wonderful model names like Carisma, Corolla, Micra and Primera were some way off.

Below: Looking down The Town along Church Street in the mid 1950s we can see the Westminster Bank on the left. Nowadays it is called NatWest. The name changed in the late 1960s. Next to it Lyon's tea rooms was a popular meeting place. Shoppers enjoyed putting their feet up for half an hour and having a good old gossip as they caught up with the latest news and scandal. There was plenty of the latter flying around in those days. In 1955 femme fatale Ruth Ellis was convicted of murdering her lover. The jury took just 25 minutes to convict her. The ex model was the last woman to be hanged in Britain. Princess Margaret, the younger sister of Queen Elizabeth II, called off her wedding with Group Captain Peter Townsend. He was divorced and there were fears of a similar royal crisis that the abdication of Edward VIII had caused. Bill Haley topped the charts with 'Rock around the clock' and helped revolutionise popular music. Housewives aired their views over the teacups before continuing their shopping sprees. They might have moved on to Pearson's, just further

down the road. The department store has been trading on this site since 1931. It opened on the former site of Enfield Constitutional Club that had been demolished in 1928. The land was once home to the 14th century Manor House. In the 15th century it belonged to the Duchy of Lancaster.

Bottom: Pearson's opened the shop on the right for business in 1931, just a few years before this scene was captured. It has been Enfield's premier department store ever since. It replaced the old Constitutional Club and redeveloped the site that had once been part of a seven acre estate. Its centrepiece, the 14th century Manor House, was a large building that had been honoured by royalty. Queen Elizabeth I once stayed there. The grand nature of the house led to it being nicknamed 'The Palace'. The name stuck and is the reason for the name of the modern shopping centre behind Pearson's. James I, the son of Mary, Queen of Scots, did it no favours. He damaged it by using some of the Palace's materials for beautifying one

of his favourite residences at Theobalds Park. In the 18th century the Palace became a boys' school and housed the Post Office in the second half of the 19th century. The present Post Office, on the corner of Little Park Gardens, did not open until 1906. Pearson's offered sophisticated shopping that was in complete contrast to the hurly burly of Market Place opposite. Ladies shopped in the store, women went to the market.

Above: Crusty rolls and tasty pastries were served at Ebben's bakery for over 100 years. The first ovens were lit in 1850 and not put out again until 1955. The George, next door, has an even longer history. The present building dates to 1895, but there had been ale flowing on this site since the early 16th century. Originally it was little more than a beerhouse. One of its early 17th century landlords was called Edward Heath. It is unlikely that he had any connection with the 1970s prime minister of the same name, but you never know! Local records show how badly this area was hit by the great plague of 1665. The George's landlord, his wife, two daughters, a grandchild and four servants all perished. By the 19th century the pub had grown in size to be a distinctive landmark on The Town. It was a wide building with a passageway through its middle. This led to stables at the rear. When the tramway reached Enfield the George became its terminus. The parade of shops to the right, just before Sydney Road, date from the same era when the George was rebuilt. Enfield House stood on the opposite corner of Sydney Road. The tall five storey building was once home to James Meyers' subscription library. In 1949 some of the kerbstones still showed white wartime markings. They were painted on to help traffic move in some safety during darkness when the blackout was in force.

Below: In 1964 the bus turning into Silver Street was one of the fleet that replaced the trolley buses. The overhead wires had gone, though some of the poles remained. Lloyds Bank is on the corner of Southbury Road and Silver Street. The open porch outside Stowell's proved to be too flimsy. A careless driver helped redevelop this corner when his vehicle smashed into the poles and carried the structure away. Enfield was still clinging to its past in the early 1960s. There had been little investment in the town centre. Many of the shops and businesses looked as if they could do with a face lift. There had been plans afoot to build an inner ring road. Investors wanted to see what happened with that before parting with their cash. When it did not materialise things began to change. The Palace Gardens Shopping Precinct brought much needed revenue to the town and shoppers returned to spend their money. Enfield's status and boundaries changed in the 1960s. It had become a borough in 1955. The London Government Act of 1963 proposed that Enfield, Edmonton and Southgate would merge to form the London Borough of Enfield. This was implemented in 1965 and Middlesex County Council was abolished. Greater London Council (GLC) was formed, though this was done away with in 1986. The powers of the GLC were then given out to the London boroughs and various joint committees.

This early postwar scene dates from c 1949. This was one of the many belt tightening years the country had to suffer after World War II. Food was rationed and petrol hard to come by. The lack of traffic on the street let people amble across the road in almost complete safety. Try and stroll across The Town at a gentle pace today and see how far you get! The pub on the left, with its Henekeys sign, became known as the Coach House in 1990. Its history goes back over 300 years. First evidence of a beerhouse on the site is dated 1698, but it might have traded before even then. It was known as The Rummer, taking its name from an old style of footed drinking glass with a large bowl. It was often elaborately etched or engraved. The word came into our language in 1654 and is German in origin. In 1854 the pub changed its name to the Railway Inn. Another name change came in 1925 when the sign over the door read as The Beaconsfield. This was in honour of the Victorian prime minister, Benjamin Disraeli. He became Earl of Beaconsfield when he entered the House of Lords. The pub reverted to being called The Rummer in 1980, but changed again a decade later. Conversation in the pub and on the trolley bus would have been about the ending of the Russian blockade of Berlin. The cost to the Allies of the airlift that began the previous summer was $200 million. Some of us muttered into our ration books about who really won the war.

Bottom: This part of Winchmore Hill is known locally as The Broadway. Findlaters, at 727 Green Lanes, was one of the wine merchants that have traded from this building since 1905. It was called Oddbins in the early part of the 21st century. The whole parade of shops dates from that era. Trade in those outlets was hit when, in the early 1990s, Sainsbury opened a supermarket nearby. The company was only returning to its roots. It opened a branch here when the parade was built, only closing in 1973. The development appeared just before the electric tramway was extended from Palmers Green. That had been ripped up 25 years before this photograph. The prominent tail fins of the saloon outside Howell's were typical of many cars produced in the early 60s. The Edmondson family built the shops and many of the Winchmore Hill properties. There is an almost identical parade that the Edmondsons built at Muswell Hill Broadway. Heading north, away from the camera along Green Lanes, would bring you to Enfield Town. The pair of houses in the distance is now used as a veterinary practice. Green Lanes was once just a country lane, set in leafy and rural surroundings - hence the name. Drovers took their animals along the track to market.

Right: The camera was pointing towards The Town, with the spire on top of Barclays Bank reaching up above the other buildings. The Ford Anglia, a popular family saloon of the 1960s, was on Southbury Road, approaching the junction with London Road and Silver Street. The photographer was standing outside the railway station with the Enfield Arms away

to his left. The pub was built in 1855, being replaced by the present mock Tudor style of establishment in 1924. It was originally known as the Enfield Arms Railway Tavern, having been built not long after the station opened. Great Eastern Railways (GER) opened its first section of the Cambridge main line in 1840 with stations at Angel Road and Ponders End. The branch line from Angel Road to Enfield Town was opened in 1849. This was just a single track line, but it marked the start of the rail era at the Nags Head Lane (Southbury Road) terminus. Great Northern Railway (GNR) brought a branch line to Enfield from Wood Green in 1871, with a terminus at Windmill Hill. GNR attracted a better class of commuter than its main rival, GER. The former company served the more middle class areas of the town that included Bycullah, Old Park and Glebe. St Onge Parade, the group of shops on the corner of Genotin Road, was built in 1932. Southbury Road was widened at about the same time.

Above: The Green, Winchmore Hill, is on the edge of the former Grovelands estate that belonged to the influential Taylor family. There was once a large pond here. Ducks swam there until 1908 when the Council filled it in. The turret on the King's Head is very similar to that on the old Nag's Head in Enfield. The pub replaced the old village inn that started life as a large pair of semide- tached houses. The present King's Head was built in 1896. Nobody uses its full title any more. But, King's Head and Railway Hotel reminds us of its transport connections. The railway came to Winchmore Hill in 1871. The station was built on Middle Road. That name changed in 1900 to Station Road. The old village fire station is to the left of the King's Head. The shops on the Green look very much the same today as they did 40 years ago. We may have The Studio on the Green and the Fountain CafÈ, but the buildings are as they were. The Green was the centre of the old village. A strong Quaker community lived here from 1688. The meeting hall in Church Hill goes back to 1790. Population grew and Winchmore Hill spread out from the Green only after the opening of the railway station and the laying of the tramway. By 1914 Highfield and Eaton Park estates were nearly complete and the shopping development on The Broadway was well established.

Below centre: The Georgian cottages on Southgate Green were built in 1780 by the Valentine Poole trust for the poor of Barnet. Architect and surveyor Michael Searles (1750-1813) designed them. We can thank Southgate Civic Trust for saving them from demolition. They had been trading as a variety of businesses, as can be seen in this 1962 photograph. After much campaigning the shops were removed and the cottages restored by Peake Estates Ltd in 1981. Barclays Bank, at no 33, has become Salcombe Preparatory School. This building is not part of the Georgian row. It was built in 1927 and replaced the old bank that was once a house belonging to Reverend Benjamin Waugh, the founder of the NSPCC. He can look down from above with a contented smile. It is very appropriate that his house is being used for the benefit of young children. The other buildings, pictured along to no 23, are flats and houses with pretty names, like Cherry Cottage at no 28. The street is now a reserved parking area, just off the A1004. It was around Southgate Green that the little hamlet of South Street grew. The centrepiece is still the Ye Olde Cherry Tree, off to the right of the cottages. It dates from the 16th century and was a coaching inn with stables where horses could take an overnight stop whilst passengers enjoyed the hospitality of the landlord.

Left: The little Mini and the Austin van take us back to a time when British cars dominated our roads. Even in 1970 a foreign car was a novelty. That scenario was soon to change. John Buckle, the respected grocer, was to see cars from Europe and the Far East parked outside the shop by 1986 when it became a branch of Cullens Stores. Buckle's had been on The Green, Winchmore Hill since before World War II. The newsagent and tobacconist lasted into the 21st century, but other businesses struggled in the face of competition from supermarkets. The antique shop replaced one such domestic retailer. Smaller grocery businesses have taken over the old Buckle shop from Cullen's. Winchmore Hill has become a desirable place to live. Inhabitants can, in part, thank the powerful Taylor family who owned the Grovelands estate. When other areas were being overrun with low cost housing, terraced properties and homes that could easily develop into slums the Taylors indulged in their own form of green belt philosophy. The family made sure that their large landholding prohibited suburban spread in late Victorian days. Much of the housing we can now see dates from the 20th century, after the Taylors had sold Grovelands. Perhaps Winchmore Hill is now beginning to show its age. However it is more that of a benevolent great aunt than a scruffy down and out relative.

Above: The shops along Station Parade, behind the bus, are still with us. A florist does good business there nowadays. Alongside it are other assorted retail outlets that include the fast food shops without which modern society cannot exist. The general view of Southgate Circus shows Chase Side running away towards Cockfosters. Barclays Bank remains, but Lee's store has been replaced by a new parade of shops. The Piccadilly Line opened between Hammersmith and Finsbury Park in 1906. The Cockfosters extension was agreed in 1930. It opened as far as Arnos Grove in 1932. The extension was completed in 1933 when Southgate, Oakwood and Cockfosters were finally linked. The creation of Southgate Circus was begun in 1931 in preparation for the coming of the Tube. It was not just the developers of the 1960s and 1970s who lacked soul. Clapboarded properties were demolished on the southern part of Chase Side. A lovely triangle of trees was sacrificed in the name of progress. There was more protest after the war over the demolition of the Grange, a fine house built in 1875. Standing on the corner of the Bourne and High Street it was home to John Bradshaw, chairman of the Taylor Walker brewery, from 1895 until his death in December 1939. The entrance to the underground station is usually a busier place than it appears in this shot. The whole scene is much more active now. Vehicles clog the roundabout and an array of traffic lights has sprung up to help the flow.

High days & holidays

A happy family life means as much as inheriting a fortune. Perhaps it is worth more. Surely no amount of money could buy the happiness shared by these parents and their daughter. Hand in hand with dad the little girl was enjoying the peaceful scene at Enfield Town Park in the 1930s. This spot has changed little in the intervening years. It is still a restful place to stroll under the spreading branches and along the pathways. On a bright summer's day people still sit on the grass and indulge in a spot of sunbathing. More active ones get out the cricket bat and practise the strokes that Bill Edrich and Denis Compton used to play. Truly energetic types run up to the coat on the ground being used as the bowler's end. Imagining themselves as Alan Moss or prancing in like JJ Warr used to in the 1950s, they deliver a tennis ball with all the determination of a Test bowler. Behind the pavilion and its cafÈ games of old man's marbles are still carried on. That description is usually given to the skilful art of playing bowls by those who have no idea of thumb bias or how to collect the jack. The parkland was formerly part of the Chase Side House Estate. The council purchased it in 1901 for £6,750, with further land being added in succeeding years.

Below: The grace and beauty of swans entrances old and young alike. The little group of people enjoying the sunshine c 1960 has stopped to admire the elegant lines of the long necked bird on the pond in Whitewebbs. It seems remarkable that these birds which can weigh up to 50 lbs find the lift to enable them take to the skies. However, you only have to see the spread of those magnificent wings to appreciate the awesome power they can release. Even the most majestic of creatures cannot resist a titbit or two. Workers often shared their lunchtime sandwiches with the swans and children came regularly to feed them from their little bags of breadcrumbs. The parkland takes its name from the house that was built in the grounds in 1791 by Dr Abraham Wilkinson. The land used to be part of the former Breton Estate. It once had a house that was occupied by the conspirators in the 1605 Gunpowder Plot to blow up the Houses of Parliament. They met in secret to discuss their plans. The estate stayed in the control of the Wilkinson family until 1900. By 1931 ownership had passed to Sir Duncan Orr-Lewis. He sold it to Enfield UDC for £23,000. The following year a municipal golf course was built. Players there were more interested in birdies, eagles and albatrosses than in swans.

Bottom: History does not record the nature of the competition that these lads had entered. Whatever it was, they had been successful. The cup they won might only have been tiny in comparison with the huge trophies that some competitions present, but to this cub scout troop it meant as much as the FA Cup. Freshly scrubbed knees were on display as they posed for the team photo. The knees belonging to the big lads in the centre were the property of Fred Hearn (l) and Sidney Collins (r). They were the leaders of the 4th Enfield Cub Scouts in the late 1920s and 1930s. Without the patience and voluntary help of such people there would have been no cubs, scouts, brownies or guides for us to enjoy. The uniforms may have changed, but the aims for the children remain much the same. Adults, keen to help youngsters develop a sense of purpose and enjoyment, organised games, practical sessions and field trips. They helped children work together and gain pleasure from teamwork. This group used to meet at the old Gordon Lane School. When the school closed in 1923 the cubs and scouts took it over. It had not been the most attractive of buildings. Some said it was dark, damp and smelly. Gordon Road was once known as Fighting Cocks Lane after a pub of that name. The name was changed in 1858 when a new road was laid on the site of the former Gordon House. A modern scout hut, dating from 1971, is the troop's present meeting place.

Left: The tables were creaking under the weight of the food at this 1954 party. The war was still within memory, but Britain was beginning to turn the austerity corner. Rationing was coming to an end. Employment was on the up and the feel good factor was returning. We rejoiced that Churchill had been back at no 10 since 1951. However, he did not feel too good about the Sutherland official portrait of him. It showed the famous old chap in a non flattering light. The painting was put away and it was discovered that his wife was so disgusted with it that she put it on the fire some years later! But we had some things to be proud of. Jim Peters nearly won the Commonwealth Games marathon, collapsing a few yards from the line. Roger Bannister ran the first ever sub four minute mile and Lester Piggott rode the first of nine Derby winners. The family in the picture had something else to celebrate. Mr and Mrs David Hawkes, out of picture at the top table, were entertaining guests on the occasion of their silver wedding. It was a double celebration. Sheila Hawkes was at the far end of the first table. Looking as pretty as a picture in her black choker, she had slipped down there to be on the shot. Sheila was born on her parents' fourth wedding anniversary, so this was her 21st party as well. The meal was held in the reception room of the White Hart, Ponders End. It is the oldest pub in the area, dating from 1627. A portrait of Judge George Jeffreys used to hang here. He was the 'hanging judge' of the 1685 'Bloody Assizes'. Roundhead troops were garrisoned here in the Civil War. The Royal Navy Association used this very room before moving to the British Legion buildings on Nags Head Road. Ponders End Brewery used to adjoin the pub, but it burned down in 1877.

Above: The now derelict Broomfield House was gutted by fire in 1984. The panorama across the lake of this once majestic mansion displays how it looked 20 years before the flames licked the half timbering that had been added between the wars. When Broomfield Park was opened to the public in 1903 the house became a borough focal point. Both national and local events were celebrated here. Wartime rallies and notable anniversaries attracted large crowds. Broomfield House was once merely a farmhouse, before being developed into a large house by 1624. The name is derived from John Broomfield, a London dyer who owned the estate in the 16th century. It passed into the hands of the wealthy Jackson family who added a grand staircase, attractive murals, chimneypieces and panelling in the 18th century. The Jacksons laid out the park with its ponds, lawns, walls and ornamental gardens. In the 1800s the Powys family remodelled Broomfield House. They improved the roads around the estate. Powys Lane, that forms the western border of the park, keeps the family memory intact. Ralph Littler, one of the men behind the drive to separate Southgate from Edmonton in 1881, lived in the house during the last 18 years of Queen Victoria's reign. When he left in 1901 the land was sold off. The house and part of the estate was bought by Southgate UDC. Since then Broomfield house has been a council school, a maternity centre and a dental clinic. In 1925 it became Broomfield Museum. The building was requisitioned by the military during World War II and used by the Medical Corps. When it was handed back in 1949 the house retained the first floor health centre.

Both pages: The more the years roll by the more difficult it will be to remember the open air swimming baths that graced the corner of Great Cambridge Road and Southbury Road. They closed in 1990 and were demolished as the millennium drew to a close. Housing and a multiplex cinema now sit above what had been a popular source of entertainment and regular meeting place since July 1932. These pictures were taken during that first summer the baths opened. They show just how much of a hit Southbury Baths became from the very first day that it opened its doors to the paying public. The water cascading down the fountain and the attractively laid out surrounds all added to the warm ambience of the place. Often people did not bother to take a dip. They were quite happy to lounge in deckchairs or loll about sunbathing and watch the world go by. Young couples shyly chatted each other up. Families played together. Men showed off their prowess on the diving board as young women giggled or marvelled at their antics. In the early days the whole concept was regarded as being sensational. Mixed bathing indeed! Whatever would the keepers of public morals think of that? The older generation was very worried about the idea when it was first proposed in 1929. A superintendent was appointed just to make sure there was no hanky panky. But when have our elders not been perturbed about the way in which the younger generation behaves? Tut-tutting is nothing new.

Enfield had a strong connection with swimming that dated back to the century before this baths opened.

The Victoria Swimming Club was established as long ago as 1887. When it held its championships at Rammey Marsh over 2,000 spectators would turn up to watch the entertainment. Later there was a small indoor heated pool, combined with public baths, at Bradley Road, Enfield Lock. Enfield Local Board built it. These boards had taken over local administration of such places as Edmonton and Enfield in 1850 from the vestries that used to be the main form of local government. In later years lady swimmers were given the privilege of using the pond at Enfield Town Park on Wednesdays. It was a big step to move from such segregation to the mixed dipping at Southbury Baths. Women had only been granted equal voting rights with men in 1928. The establishment had a lot of rethinking to do and it did not come quickly. Southbury Baths was laid out to the best of specifications.

I ts diving boards and water chutes were especially popular. Swimsuits that men and women wore were remarkably similar. One piece costumes were still the choice of the majority of men, though by the end of the decade most would be favouring shorts or trunks. By then some daring women opted for two piece costumes that were tops and shorts. The abbreviated bikini came along in 1947.

It was the railway that helped make swimming become popular. In Victorian times it helped open up the coast to townies. Day trips and longer holidays at the seaside were easier to take. Sea bathing became the new craze, so it was not surprising to see pressure put on local councils to build swimming baths where the public could practise the new popular pastime. It became an important Olympic

sport and provided the public with heroes to emulate. Several of these transferred their success from the pool to the silver screen. Johnny Weissmuller won Olympic gold in 1924 and 1928. He went on to Hollywood fame as Tarzan in a series of 12 movies. Clarence 'Buster' Crabbe played Flash Gordon and Buck Rogers on film as a result of his 1932 gold medal. Other first rate swimmers, like Esther Williams and Lloyd Bridges, used their prowess to help their acting careers. Esther starred in Busby Berkeley spectaculars and Lloyd made a TV series called 'Sea Hunt'. Swimmers showing off at Southbury Baths were often greeted with the cry, 'Who do you think you are - Johnny Weissmuller?' It usually prompted the response, 'Well it's better than looking like one of his apes!' We lost a lot of fun when the baths closed.

Grovelands was one of the many fine houses designed by John Nash. He was the Georgian and Regency architect who was responsible for London's Regent Street and Regent's Park. He also rebuilt Brighton Pavilion and redesigned St James' Park. His regular landscaping partner, Humphrey Repton, laid out the park. Walker Gray built the house on the northern side of the Bourne in 1797. Originally known as Southgate Grove it was given its present name by John Donnithorne Taylor who bought the estate in 1835. During World War I it became one of the many annexes of North Middlesex hospital. Used as a hospital for wounded soldiers it gave them treatment and surroundings in which they could convalesce after suffering the horrors of the 1914-18 conflict. On 14 June 1919 a fete was being held to raise funds for the upkeep of the house. Local townspeople happily gave their time and money to support such a worthy cause. Many of the men were still recovering from their wounds. A large proportion of those in residence were suffering from shell shock. War brought mental stresses as well as physical pain. Some of the army generals failed to recognise that. At a distance from the front line they were protected from the stark reality of life in the trenches. Shell shock was just an excuse for cowardice to them. Grovelands is now a 65 bed short stay psychiatric hospital. The former Chilean dictator, General Pinochet, was one of its most famous residents in the late 1990s.

Events & occasions

Above: Enfield's fire crew was giving one of its senior officers a good send off as the happy couple left church in the late 1920s. The rice and confetti flew over their heads as three cheers were called for. The bride was dressed in a very modern style. Not for her the formal bridal gown. She had the style of dress that would not have gone amiss on the dance floor. She looked the epitome of chic in her wide brimmed hat that still held elements of the smaller cloche style of the Charleston and flapper era. The sheer elegance of her stockings and lightly strapped shoes tell us that she knew a thing or two about fashion. The bridegroom was a lucky chap. He had got himself a stunner. The lads in the brigade were envious. 'Didn't think he had it in him' was said with grudging admiration. These were grudging times for others as well. Many thought that the cost of the upkeep of a fire service was excessive. Those were the days of the depression and money was short and unemployment high. In 1931 the council greeted a request for three full time officers and two ambulance men, costing 75s a week each, with a sharp intake of breath. When this was linked with expenditure of £1,469 on a fire pump, £370 on a fire trailer and £370 on a tender and hose there was initial resistance to such extravagance. Fortunately, it was pointed out that Enfield had suffered 151 fires that year already. With some reluctance the funds were found. The fine brass helmets worn by the fire crew were done away with in 1934. It was discovered that they tended to light up and turn the men's hair frizzy when they came into contact with electric cables!

Left: The carriage was carrying the carnival princesses and leading the procession for one of the first celebrations that Enfield had held since the war ended. The joyful mood of the children was understandable. Most of them were dressed up for the day and they were going to have fun. Behind them was a scene that strikes a chill into the bones of those old enough to remember the terror and carnage brought to London by the flying bombs. They were unleashed on the city in the final months of the war when Hitler made one last attempt to break our spirits. He failed in that plan, but succeeded in wreaking a terrible revenge on many homes and families. Mapleton Road, just off Hertford Road, was badly hit on 25 March 1945 when a V2 rocket came down. Nine houses were completely destroyed and over a hundred badly damaged. Seven people lost their lives in this single incident. The first wave of the doodlebugs, as they were nicknamed, came in June 1944, just after the D Day landings. The first missiles were coded as V1 bombs. In September a longer range version, the V2, was launched. When people heard the whine of the doodlebug it was frightening. When the noise stopped, it was terrifying. That meant that the high explosive was falling to earth close by. The house in the photograph belonged to a family who lost everything in the raid. The 15 year old daughter described how she was trapped under the heavy pressure of bricks, glass and rubble. Now in her 70s she can still recall that four people out for a walk were blown to bits. Their remains were collected in a dustbin. She had nightmares for years.

Above: The large crowd outside the North Metropolitan Electric Power Supply Company was on Lodge Drive, off Green Lanes, Palmers Green outside the newly opened Westminster Bank. The electricity offices have since closed and been replaced by a McDonald's restaurant. Such is progress. In 1927 a small brass band was playing. A clergyman was leading a memorial service. Thoughts turned to the Great War as Armistice Day was commemorated. Even nine years after 11 November 1918 when Marshal Foch accepted the German surrender on behalf of the Allies the sacrifices made by our armed forces were still fresh in people's minds. More had perished in this war than in any other the world had ever known. Ten million lay dead. Casualties among junior officers were three times higher than among ordinary soldiers. The country had lost many of those who might have become future leaders or captains of industry. Britain mourned a lost generation. As the crowd bowed its collective head in respect some of those gathered wondered what had been achieved. In 1927 British troops were in China, defending our nationals in Shanghai. Russia executed 20 Britons as spies. Vienna was rocked by revolutionary riots and in Nuremberg a crowd was heard chanting 'Heil Hitler' at a political rally. At home postal workers had their wages cut and 200 unemployed Welsh miners from the Rhondda marched on London. Army chief Lieutenant General Sir A Montgomery-Massingberd forecast another war would come within 20 years. We should have listened to him.

Above: These men were on a daytrip from St Bartholemews Hospital to the clubhouse at Enfield Golf Club. Many of the men in the photograph would have been part of the British Expeditionary Force (BEF) that suffered heavy casualties at Mons and in Flanders. The sight of crutches, slings, eye patches and heavy bandages are just a hint of the horrors these troops had faced prior to posing for this photograph on 11 April 1915. War had been declared the previous August. Cheering crowds surged onto the streets of London. They gathered in Downing Street and outside Buckingham Palace to celebrate the announcement. Field Marshal Sir John French helped the enthusiastic mood of the people. He stated that the war would be over by Christmas. With such jingoistic words ringing in their ears, young men flocked to the enlisting areas to join up. By the end of the month the 70,000 strong BEF had crossed the Channel, engaged the enemy and been thrown back at Mons. Talk of a quick victory no longer rang true. By early September Lord Kitchener, the secretary of state for war, had called for another 500,000 army recruits. His famous recruitment poster, 'Your country needs you', is regarded as the most influential advertisement of the 20th century.

Above right: The Cross Keys, pictured under the beam of the searchlight, used to stand at the southern end of The Green, next to Salmons Brook. It was one of the buildings that was able to escape the destructive sweep of the developer's arm in the 1960s. It was the last of the original pubs on Edmonton Green to survive in any form. It had a checkered career. It underwent an almost total rebuild in the early 20th century and underwent a variety of name changes. There were several

periods of closure and it eventually went into terminal decline. However, it was ironic that, having survived the area's redevelopment, it was destroyed by fire in the 1980s. During the second world war a large anti aircraft searchlight regularly shone into the sky from the rear of the pub. These carbon arc lamps became a necessary part of our defence system against the onslaught of the Luftwaffe. Night after night their beams played across the evening sky searching out the Heinkels, Dorniers and Junkers that carried loads of death and destruction for the capital and our industrial heartland. The anti aircraft batteries aimed their guns at the planes caught in the beams of light that criss-crossed the heavens. Then the ack-ack went into operation. Tracer shells marked out the path of the defenders' response to the enemy intruders. Our pilots helped knock out the threat of the bombers, but they could not be everywhere. We could do our bit from the ground.

Below: Chestnut Road was about to throw a party the like of which had not been seen for years. It was mainly women and children who would have the fun. There were very few men available to share in the celebrations. Many were still away, putting the finishing touches to the six years of war with Germany. Some of them would not be coming home at all. They had made the ultimate sacrifice. The babies on their mothers' knees might not have met their fathers yet. Other toddlers were to have a rude awakening when their dads came home. Their world, centred around mum, was not one in which they were used to hearing a gruff male voice. After demob many men found it hard to move back into a house where they were greeted as intruders. Some women had not waited as faithfully as they ought and countless marriages were sorely tested. Scandalmongers loved to spill the beans. Gossips have always taken pleasure in passing on information that can hurt. In 1938 there were 10,000 divorce cases. In 1945 it rose to 25,000. The Lord Chancellor reported in

November 1946 that there had already been 38,000 in that year, with 50,000 anticipated for 1947. But such thoughts were put on one side on VE Day in Chestnut Road. The war in Europe was over. It was time to raise a glass of orangeade and give three hearty cheers for our success.

Bottom: Peace came to a battered Europe on 7 May 1945. The following day Britain took to the streets to celebrate the victory. In London the chimes of Big Ben rang out at 3 pm and a large crowd listened to Winston Churchill's broadcast over the loudspeakers. People laughed for joy. Complete strangers hugged each other. A huge hokey cokey was danced around the statue of Queen Victoria. Every street in the country held a party just like this one at the northern end of Mandeville Road. Mums laid out cloths on the tables and raided their ration books. The aroma of freshly baked buns and cakes filled the air. Sandwiches were piled high and glasses filled to overflowing. The women swung into action to make sure that their children had an afternoon to remember for the rest of their lives. The sacrifices that had been made were for the benefit of future generations. The mums brushed their hands on their pinnies and put on frocks that had not had a joyful outing for ages. There were flags waving and bunting flying. Children made their own little party hats and sat down, ready to tuck in with gusto. Someone put a record on the gramophone and opened the living room window so that everyone could hear. 'We'll meet again' and the lovely voice of Vera Lynn echoed across the street. Similar scenes were repeated three months later when Japan surrendered. Then the bluebirds really did return to the white cliffs.

West Street lay just off Victoria Road in Edmonton. The area has been redeveloped since the date of this coronation party. It was a district that could be described as rough and ready. Certainly the residents called a spade a definite shovel. They were fierce in their loyalties, but did not stand on ceremony with those who failed to meet with their approval. It was not as tough a place as St Mary's Road, however. There the bobbies went around in twos and any cat with its own tail was a definite tourist. But the folk of West Street were famous for their neighbourliness, looking after one another like some kind of extended family. They showed that

common spirit during the war, when they pulled together helping each other out. On the day of Queen Elizabeth's coronation the whole street turned out to enjoy the occasion. Union flags were draped from every window. Gaily coloured bunting was strung across the street and fluttered in the light breeze. Some put on fancy dress and allotments were raided for blooms to put in the vases as table decorations. Behind the doors mums had slaved away baking buns and cakes. Meat paste and jam was spread liberally on the sandwiches. Jugs of lemonade appeared as if by magic. Just as miraculously they were emptied down thirsty throats within minutes of arriving at the table.

Drag out the dining chairs. Raid the church hall for some trestle tables. Dig around in the sideboard for some tablecloths. All we need to do now is block off the end of the street, get the grub out of the larder and pray for a sunny day. On 2 June 1953 we crowned a new monarch. The celebrations matched those of VE and VJ Day. This time there was no touch of sadness remembering those who could not come. We were all here to party in honour of Queen Elizabeth II. She had been born to be just another royal. As a female her rank in the pecking order of succession to the throne was expected to slip over the years. Her Uncle Edward's future children and their descendants would push her further down the list. Then came the 1936 abdication and Princess Elizabeth was catapulted to the top of the line when her father became king. Britons rallied to his support and to that of his daughter when she accepted the crown in Westminster Abbey that bright summer's day. On West Street, Edmonton, people watched the ceremony on flickering 12 inch screen black and white TV sets. Television was still a brand new medium. Only a few families had a set. It was amazing how popular these people were in 1952! Neighbours from the other end of the street greeted them like bosom buddies as they invited themselves into their front rooms. They watched with open mouths at the splendour of the scene described by ace broadcaster Richard Dimbleby.

of Silver Street and Victoria Road. Locals have been passing through the gates ever since. On 15 August 1945 they gathered by the bandstand to share in a service of thanksgiving for the end of the war with Japan. VJ Day was a happy event. The long war years had finally ended.

Top: Oompah oompah, stick it up your jumper! Even the naughtiest of boys would not have dared to shout this at the Palmadium tuba and euphonium player. The cinema opened on 24 December 1920 and was billed as 'North London's super cinema'. It was a marvellous building that originally held an audience of over 2,000. In the 1920s it held stage shows a well as films. With its stalls,

Above: The bandstand at Pymmes Park echoed to the sound of music for most of the 20th century. Bands played to audiences who gathered to listen to tunes from the shows or the classics. There were rousing Sousa marches and sometimes an ensemble would jazz it up a little. 'Alexander's Ragtime Band' or a chorus or two of 'When the Saints' soon got toes tapping. A loyal supporter of the Tudors, Cecil became Lord Burghley in 1571. He was the main adviser to Elizabeth I and served as Lord High Treasurer 1572-98. Edmonton Urban District Council, as it had become in 1894, leased part of the park in 1897, though it did not officially open until 1906. At the ceremony the chairman of the parks committee, Councillor Lemare, presented Sir Ralph Littler, chairman of Middlesex County Council, with a gold key. Sir Ralph duly inserted it into the lock of the main entrance gate at the corner

dress circle, upper circle and private boxes the Palmadium was more like a theatre in appearance. The interior's columns and facades were decorated with ornate figures. It boasted an orchestra, most of who were in costume to match the mood of the show on stage. When a silent film was showing it played music that heightened the action on the screen. The Palmadium also boasted a three pipe organ. The rest of the mainly female staff looked smart in the fashion of the decade. Situated on the east side of Green Lanes, Palmers Green it was renamed the Gaumont in 1951. Ten years later, on 25 February 1961, the projectionist played the final reel. 'The Singer not the Song' was chosen as the last film to be shown. Starring John Mills and Dirk Bogarde, it was a lengthy character drama. Based on a novel by Audrey Erskine Lindop, it told the story of a priest in an isolated Mexican town.

Above: The stage at Edmonton Summer Theatre hosted many a play and concert over the years. But it was not thespians or musicians who were the centre of attraction in June 1946. The mayor, Alderman Reid, was holding centre stage at the opening ceremony for the theatre. Alongside him is Patricia White. A local girl, she lived on Shrubbery Road, just off Lower Fore Street. Patricia was Edmonton's Victory Carnival Queen. Very nice she looked, too, in her long gown and winner's sash. Alderman Reid had the pleasant task of crowning her. Six years of hostilities, when there was not much to cheer us up, had ended. People gathered in large numbers to enjoy themselves without worrying about where the next V2 rocket was going to fall. Sports grounds saw record attendances. Cinemas were full. Theatres were jam packed for any event. In later years Eric Morley would introduce the Miss World contest and bathing beauties would have their day. Edmonton's carnival queen had no need to parade in a skimpy costume to win her title. She was elected because her charm and poise enhanced her good lucks. Patricia White did not need to show acres of flesh to prove her right.

Above right: Councillor LC Merrion, chairman of the London Borough of Enfield Highways committee, presented the Southgate coat of arms to Southgate Civic Trust in November 1966. It formerly marked the western boundary of the old borough that had been amalgamated with Enfield and Edmonton in 1965. The trust used to be called Southgate Civic Society. Now based at Winchmore Hill it has become known as Southgate District Civic Society as it has a wider brief than the N14 postal area. The town was part of Edmonton until 1881. It was once a mere hamlet on the southern boundary of Enfield Chase. As it grew up around the gate that led from where Chase Road and Winchmore Hill Road now meet, the reason for its name is obvious. Another small cluster of cottages was located by Southgate Green. Eventually, further development joined the two communities. Much of the district remained wooded and largely undeveloped until the 19th century. The first railways left Southgate alone. It was not until 1871 that the Great Northern Railway opened stations at Palmers Green and Winchmore Hill. Population had increased in the 1850s when streets were laid out and workmen's cottages appeared on Chelmsford Road and Nursery Road. But this was only small beer compared with the house building boom in the 1930s. As the 20th century began there were only 10,000 resident in Southgate. By the time of World War II the figure was six times higher.

When Princess Elizabeth became our queen, this scene was repeated in every street in the land. First of all people watched the ceremony on television. They thrilled to the splendid sight of the golden ceremonial state coach. The crowned heads of Europe were all there in their finery. From further afield marvellous figures such as Salote, Queen of Tonga, brought a real sense of joy to the official dealings of the day. This giant of a woman, with her beaming smile, was a hit with the crowds lining the processional route. When it was over Britons spilled out onto the streets for their parties. There were fancy dress competitions and variety shows provided by local bands, street entertainers and local residents. At the bottom of the picture one young man is getting ready to do his turn. His squeezebox was one of several varieties that were popular 50 years and more ago. The piano keys were played with his right hand whilst his left fingered the push buttons at the side. The accordion and the smaller concertina are 19th century inventions. Players of these instruments used to turn up at dances at village halls and on the bills of local talent contests. Nowadays they are usually limited to folk groups and Morris dancers. Many of the women in the picture were wearing headscarves. It was still thought by many that a woman was not properly dressed if she went outside bareheaded.

Logged on to customers' needs

Hertford Road and the surrounding area changed a good deal during the 20th century. It used to be full of nurseries, market gardens and orchards, and much of the traffic on the road at that time consisted of the horses and carts which took produce from here to the City of London. The journey must have been a pleasant one, not least because of the many pubs along the roadside, all with big forecourts and drinking troughs for the horses.

In 1930, Enfield Timber Company was established on Hertford Road. Then as now, the company operated from the building at the top of The Ride that was once the gate-house to Durants Arbour. Durants Arbour was the manor house at Ponders End during the 18th century; no trace of the house remains now, but from Richard Gough's description we know that it used to have a long gallery hung with family portraits including some of Judge Jeffreys, whose daughter was married to the owner of Durants Arbour. In bygone days The Ride used to be an unmade country road with a gate leading on to the main Hertford Road. When Enfield Timber acquired the site the manor house and its great barn had long since disappeared, but the gate-house had survived; since then Enfield Timber have tended to the maintenance of the old building and it is now the Managing Director's office. The land which Enfield Timber occupies had formerly been a nursery, and when the company first moved in there was a well in the middle of the timber yard. A little further down Hertford Road was another well-known timber yard belonging to Geo Wood & Sons (Enfield) Ltd, which much later on was to become part of Enfield Timber Company.

The founders of Enfield Timber Company were Mr J C Smith and Mr W Sill. Mr Smith was already established in the timber trade, having previously been in business as the Lea Valley Timber Company, and he brought a number of ex-Lea Valley employees with him to Enfield Timber. Wilfrid Sill had previously been employed as a manager of the bill posting company of David Weston, in Enfield Wash. Records from those early years have been preserved and offer the 21st century observer an opportunity to snatch a tantalising glimpse back in time; the leather-bound accounting books and ledgers, in which the company's very first transactions were carefully inscribed by hand, conjure up images of a world of meticulous clerks, copperplate script and gentlemen's agreements.

Above left: Co founder of the company Mr Wilfrid Sill. *Below:* The gate-house to Durants Arbour which now houses the Managing Director's office.

trees were felled had been liberally sprayed by machine gun fire, and the tree growth had subsequently covered the bullets.

In siting their new venture at Enfield, Messrs Sill and Smith had been counting on obtaining business from the many local factories, and this strategy proved successful. Customers in those early days included Bellings, Enfield Standard Power Cables, Enfield Rolling Mills, Ruberoids, Johnson Matthey and the Royal Small Arms Factory.

Less than a decade after the founding of Enfield Timber Company, war broke out. Factories in Brimsdown and Enfield received the attentions of the Luftwaffe, and the prospect of incendiary bombs landing in the immediate vicinity of a timber yard was somewhat alarming, to say the least. The firm therefore took the precaution of purchasing another piece of land on the opposite side of the road, so that if the yard was hit, they would at least be able to carry on trading. The risk of bombing was not the only difficulty which the business had to contend with during the war. The workforce was badly depleted when the younger members of staff enlisted in the armed forces, and those who were left found it hard to manage, especially as they too were involved in civil defence work. Wilfrid Sill himself was a Post Warden in Albany Park, near Chesterfield Road, and another employee, Les Edwards, who at the time of writing still works part-time for the company, was a Scout Cycle Messenger at the Ambulance Station at College Farm, behind Albany Pool.

However, one employee who joined the company in its very early days has offered us another perspective of the company's beginnings; as he remembers it, Enfield Timber started business with £5 worth of timber, covered with a sheet!

Another intriguing recollection has been handed down from those early days: when Russian timber began coming into this country, great care had to be taken when sawing the wood. This was because bullets were embedded in it and the saw blade was likely to be damaged. The forests from which the

Top: *Stacks of timber in the yard in the mid 1930s.*
Above left: *Timber piled against the old lodge building, mid 1930s.*

Timber, like virtually every other commodity, was rationed during the war. Most of the timber that was available was directed towards the war effort, and the firm was told what wood to purchase for the local factories.

After the war the men returned from the front, and the business slowly got back to normal. The back-up yard, having served its purpose, was sold to the local Council, and has subsequently been turned into a car park.

Right: *Tools in the saw mill.* **Top:** *Staff gather for a photograph in 1936.*

A number of amusing anecdotes have been passed down from that era, which serve to illustrate that even in those early days Enfield Timber Company was a lively and friendly place to work. Among the workforce was a certain Charlie Martin, who may well be known to readers connected with the company. As a teenager, Charlie was in the habit of climbing on the hoardings which fronted Hertford Road, along with the other youngsters who worked for Enfield Timber. On one occasion Charlie jumped down off the hoardings and landed on a six inch nail which went right through his instep, sticking out of the top of his foot. One of the older men who worked on the saw bench, Mr Swan, pulled the nail out; there was very little blood, the wound healed over nicely, and Charlie was back at work the following day.

In due course Charlie went off to the war, and after his demob he came back to his job at Enfield Timber. However, settling into civilian life stretched the young man's finances somewhat, and he found he could not afford all the things he wanted - and one thing he had set his heart on was a television. So he went to see his boss, Wilfrid Sill, to ask for a loan. Mr Sill went down Albany Road himself and made all the necessary arrangements so that Charlie could have whichever television set he wanted, and pay the money back weekly.

It was Charlie, too, who used to organise the firm's annual outing to Southend, for customers and staff and their wives. This was a popular tradition for many years; everybody used to save up for the event, and when the big day arrived they would all clamber on board the coach wearing their buttonholes and have a thoroughly enjoyable day out.

Enfield Timber has always had a very loyal workforce, with many employees giving long and devoted service over the years. Charlie Martin worked for the company for 24 years, but even this is put in the shadow by Les Edward's 30-plus years' service. At the time of writing Les is aged 77 and continues to work part-time in the office. Wilfrid Sill's wife also maintained an active involvement in the day to day running of the firm; at the time of writing she is in her nineties, and is still keenly interested in the business.

Joinery was always an important part of Enfield Timber's activities, and in 1965 Enfield Joinery Works was set up to concentrate on this aspect of the business.

Above: A letterhead dated 1939. Below: The interior of the lodge in 1938.

Enfield Joinery Works went on to become a major sawmilling operation, and at its height was the second largest hardwood sawmiller in the south east of England, producing 100 cubic feet every ten minutes. In more recent years, however, the manufacturing focus of the company has shifted to the production of non-standard fire doors, and trades as Enfield Speciality Doors.

Nineteen sixty-five was also the year in which the second generation of the Sill family officially entered the business - though some of the staff remember Nigel visiting his father's timber yard as a little boy, and showing quite an interest in the timber. Nigel favoured a hands-on approach; having achieved his AIWSc qualification, he worked his way through every area of the mill to get a working knowledge of all the machinery and gain a thorough understanding of the different aspects of the timber industry. One of the administrative challenges of those days was the mainte-nance of timber stock levels throughout the year when most of the ports in Scandinavia, Russia and Canada were frozen from winter until June. It was therefore necessary to build stocks up during late autumn and early wintertime. Most of the timber came into the Surrey Commercial Docks and a gang of men was employed especially to unload lorries all day long; these, of course, were the days before mechanical handling. By the time winter set in, stocks of timber

would have reached a height of up to 30 feet; by the following spring stocks would be running low, and the company would be waiting for June, when the ice would melt.

Nigel Sill took Enfield Timber over upon his father's death in 1981, and the following year he bought the nearby firm of Geo Wood & Sons (Enfield). Run by Mr Stan Wood, Geo Wood & Sons was famous for its range of hardware and ironmongery as well as being a very highly respected timber merchants. Mr Wood wished to retire, and so the business became part of Enfield Timber; the retail and trade shop was incorporated in the Hertford Road site, and today continues to sell everything connected with timber - hinges, handles, nails, screws, lacquers, varnishes, paints, timber protections and treatments, adhesives and so on - so that builders can enjoy the convenience of purchasing everything they require in one visit.

*Right: The firm's 1935 lorry retained for advertising purposes. **Below:** George Wood and Sons pictured in 1984.*

already enjoyed tremendous success and its potential for future growth in the 21st century is immense.

In December 1988 the company acquired the property next door at number 25 Hertford Road. These premises had formerly been occupied by a printing company, C B Russell & Son. Enfield Timber converted them into an additional display and sales area, and the range of timber-related items which the firm had inherited from Geo Wood & Son was transferred to this site. However, this arrangement was subsequently found to be unsatisfactory as it did not

The next major step in Enfield Timber's development came about in 1985, when a sister company called Enfield Speciality Doors was established. This branch of the business is based half a mile away from the Hertford Road site, in a factory with an acre of land, and specialises in the manufacture of fire doors. The company has continually invested in the latest machinery, which today means a computer controlled router and other state-of-the-art equipment which Wilfrid Sill could only have dreamed of. Enfield Speciality Doors has become a truly international operation, supplying fire doors for various hotel complexes in Saudi Arabia and sending employees to America for training; it has

make efficient use of the premises. The retail trade was re-incorporated into the timber yard, but the company retained ownership of the adjacent premises; at the time of writing they are leased out to a local glazier.

It is well known in Enfield that Nigel Sill has another passion besides timber: he is very interested in steam engines.

Top: *The Finnish Kana class steam engine arriving at the yard in the early 1990s.*
Above left: *Just a small part of the showroom display in 1985.*

In 1992 he had the opportunity to save a number of Finnish steam engines from the scrapyard, and he had them shipped to this country. His original plan was to operate them in a theme park in Cornwall, but when the recession set in these plans became unrealistic and had to be abandoned. One of the steam engines was put onto a low loader and delivered to the timber yard, where it was smartened up and given a new coat of paint. The engine has a long-standing connection with the timber industry as it was used in Finland to shunt timber between the various timber companies and the docks. This particular class of engine was called the Kana class; Kana is Finnish for Hen, and the engines were so called because of their constant back-and-forth shunting movements. It is now used as an advertising symbol for Enfield Timber. Nigel Sill's interest in steam locomotives is shared by many, and the power of steam will never lose its appeal for those who remember the heyday of the Great Eastern Railway and all the magnificent engines which used to operate on Britain's rail network. Equally, many youngsters are fascinated by steam engines, and the local schoolchildren are fortunate in having a chance to visit the real live steam engine at Enfield Timber when they learn about modes of transport through the years. Another of the

engines which Nigel acquired at the same time was the largest steam engine ever made in Finland, and this has been placed on display at Long & Somerville's builders' merchants yard, situated just by Southbury Station in Enfield, on the line from Liverpool Street Station to Broxbourne.

Enfield Timber has contributed a great deal to life in Enfield over the years, and will continue to do so. Despite numerous offers from competitors, it has remained an independent company in the ownership of the family which founded it. Generations of local people have enjoyed secure employment there, and in return the experience and the friendly, helpful approach of the loyal workforce is an important factor in the firm's success.

Right: *An aerial view of the firm.*
Below: *Mr and Mrs Sill in 1974. Both Mr Sill's enjoyed many years driving sports cars.*

The company has grown into one of the largest stockists of hardwoods in the local area, with one of the biggest sawmills, and a shop selling an exceptionally wide range of the best building products including security products, ironmongery and brassware, sheet materials, insulation, electric and hand tools and many hard-to-get-items; while fire doors manufactured by Enfield Speciality Doors are shipped all over the world. Computer systems, modern machinery and up-to-date storage and display systems have been installed to ensure that customers receive the best possible service, but a traditional sales policy has been retained, with a tradesman's counter to offer help and advice, and staff who take a professional interest in clients' projects and make it their business to attend to the individual needs of each and every customer. Virtually any moulding can be machined for skirtings, dado rails, and architraves, and carcassing timber can be cut to any length. Deliveries are arranged promptly and made by the

firm's own fleet of lorries. Customers range from major building companies undertaking major projects in the area, to landscape gardeners, to DIY enthusiasts; all receive the same high level of service, and all are likely to return time after time, and recommend Enfield Timber to their friends.

The company is also committed to sound environmental management practices, so customers can be sure that all the timber they purchase from Enfield Timber is of the correct quality and has been felled from sustainable forests, without damage to the environment. In short, Enfield Timber is doing everything it can to ensure that its staff, its customers and the environment at large can enjoy a successful and secure future!

Top: A picture of some of the firm's staff in the 1990s.
Above: Nigel Sill, Mary Brown and Les Edwards celebrating Mary's retirement in 1991.

On the move

Above: The British public loves a good crash. It must be part of our ghoulish nature. Why else would a crowd gather to look at a 1930 ambulance sticking through a set of railings above New River? These days drivers rubber neck on motorways when they see an accident on the opposite carriageway. They do not stop to help, just slow down to ogle. In so doing they add to the dangers, but it still happens. Obviously some things never change. This crowd has not collected to help. It is probably hoping that the ambulance topples all the way in. This accident could not happen now. Opposite Enfield Town railway station this part of the river is now covered over and used as a car park. New River is really a canal. It was Hugh Myddleton who had the idea to build it. In the early 17th century the Thames was badly polluted. Drinking water was in short supply. New River was constructed to carry water from the springs near Ware to the reservoir at Clerkenwell. When it was first cut in 1613 the river came into Enfield from Cheshunt, under Bullsmoor Lane and Turkey Street. The present course between Turkey Street and Tenniswood Road dates from 1859. It runs through the Willow housing estate. Most of the loop has been retained for ornamental purposes, though parts of it were silted up and covered in green algae for a long time. The Enfield Arms can be seen in the background. It was later rebuilt and its present appearance dates from 1924.

T his is South Street, Ponders End, towards the junction with High Street. The area is still recognisable, though the bottom end is no more. It was demolished in the late 1960s and early 1970s to make way for the planners' dream of that era, the tower blocks. Pictured outside CW Head's sweets and tobacconist's shop, this group had hired a bus to take them on a jolly boys' day out. They were nearly all dressed in three piece suits. Some had Albert or hunter watches in their waistcoat pockets, with gold or silver fob chains keeping them safe. Wristwatches were still in their infancy. Their various headgear, homburgs, trilbies, fedoras and flat caps, gave away their pecking order on the social ladder.

However, they had a common purpose. Today was Derby Day, 2 June 1920. They were off across the border into deepest Surrey for the racing at Epsom. The biggest betting of the day would take place on the main race. The Derby is named after Edward Stanley, 12th Earl of Derby and was first run in 1780. It was run on Wednesdays until recent years when sponsors and television had it switched to a Saturday. Major Giles Loder's Spion Kop won the 1920 race. On the way home winners and losers toasted each other with bottles of brown ale that had been clanking under the back seat on their outward journey. There were a few thick heads by the time they got back home. They set off as jolly boys and came back merry.

Above: Charles Holden was a trend setting architect. He designed a number of the stations on the underground Piccadilly Line. Photographed on 1 February 1934, Southgate Station had a futuristic look, light years ahead of its time. Designed by CH James, Holden was as consultant. The building was given listed status in 1971. Contrast its sleekly sculpted lines with the archaic NS type no 29 bus. It is as if the scene had been affected by some form of time warp. Either that or the photographer had been helping himself to a few draughts of Dewar's Scotch being advertised between the bus decks and then spliced together two scenes from different eras. The old bus had its driver's cab outside the main body. That helped accentuate the feeling of antiquity. London General Omnibus Company moved the no 29 terminus from Wood Green to Southgate Green in 1912. When the first bus ran in Southgate on the 'General' route it had solid tyres. That would have kept the passengers' eyes open as they were bumped around on their journey home. It took three sturdy horses to pull the bus up Alderman Hill and Cannon Hill! Once public transport had its say on a large scale, rural Southgate was no more. Trams ran in New Southgate from 1907 but never reached Southgate because of its hills. Buses did not supersede them until 1938, four years after this photograph was taken. By then the builders had cashed in on the further growth encouraged by the opening of Southgate Station. By 1939 the town was built up as far north as Bramley Road.

Above right: The Town has changed little since 1938. Only cosmetic differences can now be seen. The tramlines and overhead cables have gone. The nature of the businesses has changed. Traffic lights and a one way system have appeared, but that is about all. The junction with Silver Street to the left, London Road to the right and Southbury Road straight on is very much as it ever was. Pizza Hut and the Woolwich are now on the corner behind the bus, but the place remains unmistakable. This was one of the final journeys this no 29 tram was to make. The decision to phase out this form of transport was made in 1934. Trolley buses took over the tram routes four years later. The tramlines were ripped up, but the overhead cabling was retained as much of it was used to relay power to the trolleys. They were initially described as trackless trams, but the name never really stuck. Americans called them all streetcars. They could never use the different nuances of the English language properly. Many British towns and cities phased out their trams in between the war years and experimented with trolley buses. Both styles of transport were inflexible as they had to be attached to the overhead cables. As motor car ownership increased and town centres became clogged up, trams and trolleys only added to the congestion. Motor buses just had to replace them.

Below: When did you last see a lad wearing short trousers? In 1935 every boy wore them. Most schools banned long trousers until a child was well into double figures or had reached a certain height. Scabby knees were as much a part of a school uniform as a blazer, collar and tie. This couple was on board the no 29 tram to Tottenham Court Road. A no 329 bus covers the modern route, though it only goes as far as Turnpike Lane. Reid's Special Stout was a particularly heady Watney's brew that was popular with older drinkers. Trams had been running in the borough since the latter part of the 19th century. In 1878 the North London Tramways Company was set up. The first trams were horse drawn and proceeded at a leisurely pace. A depot was established at Tramway Avenue and the first journeys were made in 1881 from Stamford Hill to Ponders End. For a short time in the late 1880s steam powered trams ran in Ponders End and Edmonton. For a few years there was an attempt to replace horses with steam power. Those new trams turned out to be too heavy for the tracks and they frightened the horses that pulled conventional traps and wagons. North Metropolitan Tramways returned to horse power in 1891 until electrification took place in 1904. There was a great deal of sentiment displayed in 1938 as people waved goodbye to the last tram. North Metropolitan Tramways took over the administration of the service in 1891, but was replaced by Metropolitan Electric Tramways 11 years later. Barclays Bank is the imposing building beside the tram in the picture. It is still there, on the corner of The Town and Market Place. The Tottenham and Edmonton Gas Company opened the building to the left in 1914. In 1937 it was taken over by Burton's and is now home to Bradford and Bingley.

Bottom: Large crowds gathered outside the George in The Town in May 1938. They had come along in droves to witness the last tram journey ever to be made in Enfield. Since the first horse drawn tram had rattled along its track to Lower Edmonton in 1881, Enfield had enjoyed the convenience of this style of public transport. The tracks soon reached Ponders End High Street when, in 1882, Major General CS Hutchinson declared the tram to do be a safe way to travel. He was a senior inspector for the Board of Trade. It was lucky that Enfield residents did not realise he was the same man who had granted a safety certificate to the Tay Bridge in 1878. We all now know what happened to that! Trams ran through Enfield Town from 1909 onwards.

The camera was pointing from London Road north along Silver Street in 1956. Travel further along that road and you now come to the modern civic centre. Around there the road becomes known as Baker Street. Halfway along the Silver Street parade of shops to the right you can find Blake and Horlock, the funeral directors. Specially sombre funeral corteges, with a horse drawn hearse, sometimes stand outside the door. The black and purple coach coverings and beautifully plumed headdresses of the horses create an impressive and dignified sight. This part of town has a number of financial institutions gathered close together. The photographer was close to where the HSBC now operates. To his right was the 1937 National Provincial Bank. Lloyds (now Lloyds TSB) was on the corner of Silver Street and Southbury Road. It was redeveloped with extended offices behind in the early 1970s. There is also a further small office on the opposite side of Silver Street. The billboard above Defiance, advertising Andrews' Liver Salts, was a timely reminder to those who had supped too well the night before. A spoonful of the powder into a glass of water turned it into a fizzing brew that settled the stomach and cleared the head.

Right: The Goat was built at the bottom of Forty Hill in 1929. Instead of the Wolseley sitting outside the pub's front door there would once have been a pony and trap or coach and four. This mock Tudor fronted inn replaced the old Goat, also known as the Goat Tavern, further up the road, on the corner of Goat Lane, that had been serving ale since the early 18th century. There is a record of one William Senk being its landlord in 1729. The style of frontage of the present pub is a common one around the town. The Goat is built on the site of an old pond that used to be home to ducks that waddled into it from the green. The sunken garden at the back of the pub is where there used to be a gravel pit. As this area is bordering on the green belt and Enfield boasts an active preservation society it is to be hoped that some of the more attractive buildings and sights around town can be protected. Goat Lane is an extension of Baker Street that leads northward from Enfield Town. Since 1969 it has not been possible to get up Baker Street to Forty Hill as the road was cut off and housing renumbered. Buses, like the standard RT, have not had a terminus here since 1971. This postwar bus, seen here in the mid 1960s, was a robust and reliable vehicle. Younger drivers were not keen on it as it had no heating. The replacement vehicles in the following decade were more acceptable to their chilled fingers. Unfortunately, even though more sophisticated, they were less reliable as good runners in cold weather.

Below: The first awnings on Southbury Road, next to Lloyds Bank, used to belong to Grout's saddler's and ironmongery store. Lloyds extended its premises to include this shop about 1970. The picture dates from the mid 1930s. Southbury Road had been widened in 1932 to cater for the rise in traffic and to help trams and cars exist side by side more easily. Part of the Nag's Head had been demolished to make way for the redevelopment. To our modern eye there is little activity on the roads. But, nearly 70 years ago, the amount of traffic warranted a bobby on point duty. Driving standards could at best be described as carefree. The number of accidents was high in comparison with the level of car ownership. The government was horrified to learn that 127 people died on the roads in a single week during early 1934. On 28 March a comprehensive set of measures to improve road safety was included in the Road Traffic Bill. All new drivers had to take a driving test. Pedestrians could be prosecuted for walking dangerously. Speed limits were imposed in towns. Plans were made to copy a successful Parisian experiment with pedestrian crossings. Leslie Hore-Belisha was the minister of transport given the job of overseeing the changes. He was the Secretary of State for War when hostilities broke out in 1939. However, it is with the flashing beacons that stand by the first crossings he introduced that his name has forever been linked.

Shopping spree

Vicarage Farm is still there on Hadley Road, but the dairy is no more. It is now a restaurant. In 1911, on the corner of Holtwhite's Hill, E Fitz did good business from 90 Chase Side. It sold dairy products from its own farm as well as those made from milk collected elsewhere. Horse drawn wagons lumbered along the country lanes. As they reached a farm entrance the drivers would lift up the milk churns left out for them and drop off the previous day's empties. Then the clanking load made its way to the dairy to be turned into butter, cheese, rennet and junket or simply be bottled for our daily use at home. These were days that none of us can recall. Enfield in the early 20th century had one fifth of the population it has now. Industry and agriculture sat side by side. To the east of the town, Lee Marshes had some of the area's best grazing land. There were market gardens and orchards in abundance. Row upon row of large greenhouses could be seen in large numbers right up until the second world war. There was, and still is, good farmland to the north and west of the town as well. Off the Ridgeway, along Hadley Road, the Fitz's Vicarage Farm had neighbours at Park Farm, Parkside Farm and Ferry Hill Farm. As the century drew on small farm dairies gave way to large companies. Fitz closed the business in 1938.

Above: Bush Hill Parade, Village Road was built in 1929-30. The parade is pictured as it looked in 1931. The shop at the far left is home to a chemist today, just as it was 70 years ago. The area had been expanding since the 1870s and was very much an arty-crafty region. As the middle classes settled here it helped the district gain a select reputation. Bush Hill Park is the site where many Roman remains were uncovered in the 1970s. However, whatever settlement there was here 2,000 years ago was discontinued for a very long time. At the start of the 19th century there were no houses on Lincoln Road and it was a place that development had passed by. William Mellish owned a large part of what became Bush Hill Park. He lived in a mansion on what is now called Ringmer Place, near the golf course. After his death the land and house went through several sets of hands before the estate was broken up for development. The well heeled moved into the large properties built along Wellington Road and Village Road. The wide roads with their avenues of trees were more like a French boulevard than suburban Middlesex. Just after the middle classes began populating Bush Hill Park the railway came along. This encouraged developers to build The Avenues and the Cardigan Estates in the closing years of the 19th century.

Above right: FW Woolworth and Co Ltd is a grand sounding name. No one used it then and no one uses it now. In the States it was the original five and ten cent store. In Britain, Woolies it was and Woolies it will always be. Selling a wide variety of cheap and cheerful goods, it has been a store you could guarantee to find on any high street in any town in the country. Pick 'n' mix sweets for the kids, cheap packs of bathroom cubes and talc for gran's birthday and stinging aftershave for Uncle Walter were the order of the day. Take your purchase to the counter and you could guarantee the shopgirl said, 'How much is it, love?' How many times in the days before CDs have you bought an LP record of someone else singing cover versions of the hits of the day, as the real things were too expensive? By the time you'd played it half a dozen times, didn't you wish you'd saved up for the original? This branch was photographed at Palmers Green triangle in the 1920s. America's cents were translated into our pennies, but the message remained the same. Woolworth catered for those on limited budgets. It was not classy, but it was practical. The company opened its first branch in England in 1909. The Liverpool outlet was the start of a chain that covered the whole of the country within two decades.

Below: In the 1950s Dale's department store held pride of place on the corner of Balham Road, Edmonton Green. This privately owned business catered for the town's needs until 1970. It was then swept away, along with so much else, in the redevelopment purge of that era. After World War II much of Edmonton was in a run down condition. Despite the building of the council estate near Victoria Road and the private developments around Church Street in between the wars, there was a major housing shortage in the 1950s. The council organised the restructure of the town, a programme that continued throughout the 1960s. New housing replaced many of the Victorian homes that had become dilapidated. Blocks of flats appeared, towering above the skyline. Edmonton Green Shopping Centre was rebuilt from 1968. Dale's was but one of a number of businesses that bit the dust. For years it had been the place to come for household items, furniture and floor coverings. Many an Edmonton home boasted a three piece suite bought from here. But there was no sentiment in the hearts of the developers. They did not worry themselves with people who enjoyed browsing amongst the household goods that Dale's had to offer. Concrete blocks and traffic flow were the order of the day. The demolition ball swung into action. It knocked down a slice of history along with the bricks and mortar that came crashing down.

Bottom: Market Square was heaving with customers at its Saturday market. Since the 1970s it has been open three days per week. Before then traders only set up their stalls on Saturdays and on Christmas Eve. In 1303 Edward I granted the Lord of the Manor the right to hold a weekly market. The parish authorities created Market Place in 1632 on the site of a house known as The Vine. Its success led to increased trade and prosperity for a time. But, it went into decline in the 18th century. It was not revived with any success until the latter years of the following century. The Rialto Cinema, at the left of the picture, closed in 1971. The Taylor Walker brewery owned the King's Head. Walker was a famous sporting name in the area. The family was a big name in 19th century cricket, almost rivalling the mighty Graces. Southgate Cricket Club plays its home games at the Walker Ground. St Andrew's is the parish church of Enfield. The eye above the tower window is the clock face; it moved there from lower down in 1910. The church dates mainly from the 14th and 15th centuries, though one part has links with the 13th century. The Domesday Book (1086) makes reference to there being a priest living in the area, so religious links with this site may be even older. Inside visitors can find a magnificent organ case and various fine monuments.

Below: You could not move in the Market Place on Saturdays in 1950. Shoppers were packed like sardines as they tried to get a bargain from the cheery stallholders. The traders bantered with their customers, but could not spare each one too long as there were plenty more waiting to be served. The couple trying to cross the road were using the Belisha crossing. It was not until 1951 that black and white markings appeared on the crossings to help drivers spot them more easily. The pattern brought the immediate nickname of zebra crossing and the name stuck. Either side of the market stood Barclays Bank and Burton's menswear shop. Bradford and Bingley has since ousted the tailor from whom men got their demob suits after the war. Market Place used to host two annual fairs, but they were discontinued in the late 1800s. The market had ceased to function in the first part of that century and was not revived until just over a century ago. The eight teak columns of the octagonal Market House (1904) were put in place in honour of the coronation of Edward VII that took place two years earlier. The structure replaced the old market cross that had been there since 1826. It had fallen into disrepair and was taken away by Edward Augustus Bowles. He was a well respected figure in the world of botany. Gussie, as he preferred to be known, took the cross to his home at Myddleton House, now part of Lee Valley Regional Park.

Right: John Collier was always the window to watch. That was the gist of adverts for the tailor who was popular in the early 1960s. Across the way, on the other side of The Town, Dunn & Co was a major rival. The two tone Vauxhall parked near the pedestrian crossing was one of a series of models that aped American styling. Cars began to start appearing in the showrooms painted in a host of bright colours. Some had large rear fins. Unfortunately these turned out to be rust traps and motorists had their fingers burned as they had to shell out on body repairs or see the secondhand value plummet. The van that has turned out of Sydney Road can still perform that manoeuvre today. The cars heading towards it have to find a different way round. In 1970 Enfield's answer to traffic congestion was to introduce a one way system. The old trolley bus poles that carried the cables that sparked and crackled with electric power for the pantographs had yet to be taken away. They were just a reminder of the form of public transport that left our streets in 1961 after 23 years' service. The heartland of the town's shopping area was all along The Town and into Church Street. It is much the same today, though the emphasis has moved to the left of Church Street, as we look at it. Palace Gardens Shopping Precinct opened in 1982 and took a lot of the business that used to be carried on in the shops that we can see in this picture.

The woman in the neat suit on the left has had her attention caught by something going on across Church Street. Perhaps the man from the Pru was trying to attract her in to sell her a policy. In the mid 1950s people used to get the insurance man calling round to the house. The British are careful to save for a rainy day.

Modest weekly contributions to little life insurance policies built up small nest eggs for the future. They had slim books in which the insurance man recorded each payment. He entered them up in his own pocket book before transferring them to a larger ledger at home or back at the office. When granny died the agent would bring the cheque round

personally. People in the 21st century talk glibly of ISAs, TESSAs and PEPs. They insure their lives using push button phones. Press one if you want to arrange cover, two if you want to cash in a policy and three if you are totally confused. There seems to be no way you can actually get to speak to someone. The Post Office is just west of the Prudential

Assurance office. It has been there since 1906. Howard's, on the other side of Little Park Gardens, at 31 Church Street deals in electrical appliances. They were just beginning to be on every home's must have list. Labour saving devices and appliances that entertained us became part and parcel of everyday life. They used to be luxuries.

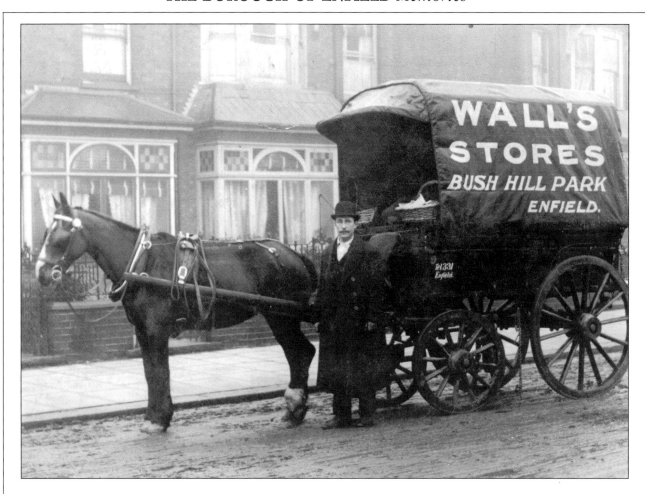

Making a living

These fine bay fronts were built on Edenbridge Road, Bush Hill Park in 1903. Wall's Stores and the butcher's shop of R Wall and Son were at 4 Station Parade, St Mark's Road. The shop was built in 1908 and the photograph dates from just before World War I. Housewives placed their orders at the store. Staff made them up and packed them into boxes or baskets. Then the delivery wagon was loaded up and the horse trundled the food off along the streets to the shoppers' homes. A big shopping expedition needed such backup. Public transport did not reach all Enfield's outskirts on a frequent basis. The motor car was in its infancy and

housewives could not manage to carry home everything they had bought. Lads took smaller loads on bikes, with their cycle baskets crammed with pies, chops and legs of lamb. They were very popular with local dogs. They pursued the delivery boy with great enthusiasm, hoping to run off with a string of sausages in their teeth. The man in charge of the horse in this camera shot regarded his work seriously. He was dressed in a smart overcoat and derby hat. He had a commercial business to conduct. It was important to him to treat it professionally. It must have been a bumpy ride for him, sitting up behind the horse above the boneshaker wheels.

Below: H Gomm and Son had a butcher's shop at 2 The Town in the 1920s. The business closed in 1934. The old shop is now part of the Woolwich and Pizza Hut building that occupies the corner of The Town where Southbury Road and London Road meet. The leaves were still on the tree as this delivery boy was taking a small order out to a customer. But there must have been a nip in the air. He made sure that he was well wrapped up. Horse drawn transport was still an important part of town and country life 80 years ago. Lorries and vans did not take over completely until the late 1920s and early 1930s. Although the petrol engine was more practical the romance of the noble steed was hard to challenge. Unfortunately, romance had little place in business. As this horse and cart went gently along the road the world outside was changing. After World War I Britain was to find its place challenged as a super power. America's influence grew ever large. Revolution in Russia had changed the order of things in that great northern nation. To the east the distant empires of Japan and China would become more powerful. Britain even struggled to keep promises to its own people. The country did not become the land fit for heroes that the government had guaranteed. Unemployment grew. Slum housing provided poor living conditions and there was real trouble when miners' wages were reduced, prompting the 1926 general strike.

Bottom: Yorkshire House, where Gardner and Burgess carried out their coal merchants' business, is still in place on Chase Side, Enfield Town. It is not full of invoices for nutty slack any more as it is now a private house. That is a fairly recent development as the coal wagons ran from here until about the late 1970s. Gardner and Burgess set up their business in 1906. They went their separate ways in 1924 when the firm became known as just Burgess. This 1910 photograph acts as a reminder of the days when coal mining was one of our most important industries. So much depended on it. Coal was used to support iron and steel plants, the potteries, power stations and our own domestic fireplaces. The railways and mighty steam ships relied on the rich deposits our miners hacked from the bowels of the earth. Gardner and Burgess wagons used to trundle through the streets, piled high with hundredweight sacks, to keep us warm on the long winter nights. The coalman tipped the coal into bunkers and chutes. He left the empty sacks outside so that the careful housewife could count that the right number had been delivered. Many of our homes had kitchen ranges fuelled by coal, so we needed it to cook our food as well as taking the chill off our houses. They were days of long toasting forks being pushed into the fire to brown crumpets and muffins for tea. We got dressed in a morning by the still warm embers of last night's fire.

Margaret Neale lived on Mitchell Road in 1938. It is now just yards from the thousands of vehicles that thunder along the North Circular Road each day. The horse drawn milk float would not have a chance trying to make deliveries in this day and age. Even in the immediate prewar years motorised vans and floats had largely sent horses out to grass. Perky and pretty as a picture, little Margaret posed for the camera. In her white ankle socks, sandals and summer dress she might have fallen off the lid of a chocolate box. Even at her tender age she knew how to be coy if it meant she could get her way. Her sister, now Janet Lane and a member of Southgate District Civic Trust, had also smiled nicely at the milkman. He agreed to let Janet snap young Margaret for the family album. Little girls have always been able to twist dads round their little fingers. It was good practice for when they had a favour to ask of another male. Men are always suckers for little imps and their winsome smiles. It doesn't change when they get older! The Express Dairy was not going to match its name on this day. Not only was the horse going to proceed at the rate it wanted, the milkman was not going anywhere until the photo shoot was completed. Did Margaret and Janet carry on charming all the chaps they met? You can bet your life on it.

Above: Camera Craft Ltd was established in Palmers Green in the early 1920s. It is still on the corner of Osborne Road and Green Lanes today. Stored inside what was once a private house with a shop front added later is a historical goldmine. In the storerooms and lofts are images, plates and negatives of a century of memories. Faces and scenes from the past stare out from the prints and slides reminding us of times when we were young and granddad was but a lad. The company had not been long established in 1923 when the staff posed for this photograph outside the 'Work Rooms'. Edgar Chard founded Camera Craft at 1 Osborne Road. He is the chap peeking round the shoulder of the woman seated second left. Who the little lad on the wall belonged to is not clear. Sitting next to Edgar is Cyril Hornby. He was one of the original partners in the firm. Betty Hurst sat at the left on the front row. She was to serve the company faithfully until 1970. When she retired a piece of company history went with her. She was Edgar's secretary for all that period. She was such an integral part of

Camera Craft that when someone wanted to know any background on an item he was told, 'Ask Betty. She's bound to know.' 1928 - 1931, Cyril Hornby ran the shop at 39 Church Street, Enfield, which traded as Hornbys from 1931 to 1969. Edgar Chard died in 1986. The inheritance he left is for the benefit of all keen students of life as it was in the 20th century.

Top: The good, the bad and the ugly. The reader can choose which is which! It would be far too insulting to Mr Hooper and his staff to allocate an individual description. The mobile grocery business was based at 34 Halifax Road, one of the houses behind the van. A plaque on the wall identifies these as being Bruce Cottages. They were originally built as low cost housing for the working classes. HA Hooper's grocery business, founded in 1929, was the forerunner of the modern supermarket. As well as packets of tea, boxes of biscuits and tins of corned beef you could pick up all manner of odds and ends. Shoelaces, polish and light bulbs were among the assorted range of goods that people might just happen to find being carried. In a grocer's shop it was always worth asking because the proprietor just might have that little something you needed round the back somewhere. The mobile van could not carry quite that same range, but Mr Hooper always listened to his customers. If a housewife requested an item that was not on board he made sure it was there on his next trip. Those were times when personal service was part and parcel of doing business. The van drivers and delivery boys regarded customers as their friends as well as being part of the business. It was a slower age and one where we had chance to pass the time of day and take an interest in one another's welfare.

The mayor of Enfield sat at the wheel of the 1928 fire brigade appliance. He was only posing for the photograph. The brave lads in uniform did the real work. Their fire station was opposite the Stag Inn at Little Park Gardens and is now a bus turn around. The Stag had developed from an 18th century cottage that became just a little beerhouse in 1847. The fire crew could slake their thirst there after a tour of duty, but never beforehand. This grand set of chaps was virtually all volunteer. It was not until 1930 that the town would see regular full time firemen. The force began as a volunteer brigade in 1880. Other firefighting groups in Britain were often linked with insurance companies in the early days. The growth in population and the rise of industry in the 19th century brought added hazards of fire in crowded settlements and dangerous factories.

Insurance claims, not to mention a certain level of self inflicted arson, encouraged the companies to fund fire brigades. They were protecting their interests rather than those of the local population. But, it was a start. Gradually local councils took over the administration of these brigades. The Enfield force started with an old 1840 hand cranked appliance. Kept in a damp shed, its hoses were mouldy and the wheels were riddled with dry rot. It was in such a state of poor repair that the wheels collapsed under it during one turn out. There were two Enfield volunteer forces in the early 1900s. By the end of World War I both brigades suffered from equipment that had fallen into disrepair. The surviving brigade, pictured here, was getting back on its feet with its smartly uniformed force and handsome fire engine.

Above: The age profile of Enfield's firefighters during the second world war was high. Several of these men had seen active service in the first world war, but were too old to re-enlist when the balloon went up in 1939. Anxious to serve their country once again they volunteered their services for a variety of civil defence organisations. Some became firewatchers or air raid wardens. Others became part of the Home Guard. Some of the men in this photograph volunteered their services to the fire station at Holtwhite's Hill. The building was modern. It had only opened in June 1936, at a cost of £42,000. Sir Henry Bowles performed the opening ceremony at the station that was the pride and joy of Enfield's fire service. It was equipped with the world's most up to date fire alarm. As the bombs rained down on north London in the early 1940s its resources were tested to the full. From the onset it had a professional fireman in charge and he led his team with great skill and efficiency. Seven of the station staff were given such a good grounding that they went on to senior posts in other brigades within just a few short years. There were also plans to build another new station at Carterhatch Lane in 1938, but these were put on hold and not resurrected until the 1960s. Holtwhite's Hill station closed in that same era and is now the HQ of the British Legion.

Bottom: The headgear in the photograph shows the variety of fashion and formality available to men in 1930. On the right and in the background are two young lads. Those caps they are wearing shaded their eyes and covered half of their ears to boot. There were right places and right times for everything. The hairstyle and moustache of the chap giving the speech are reminiscent of someone else who would be good at giving speeches. Herr Hitler was just three years away from becoming Chancellor of Germany when this picture was taken. This British orator was far removed from the person who became the most vilified man of the century. Our chap had come to speak about caring for the community as he was addressing the crowd about the bravery of the local fire-fighters. The man to the right is wearing a natty felt homburg and to the left a seriously dressed David Frank Hawkes is sporting a fine bowler hat. Mr Hawkes was Enfield's first regular fire officer. When the brigade turned out the rest of the crew used to appear rushing up the street from shops, houses and offices as they were all volunteers. He lived in Stag Cottage, which was attached to the Stag Inn, just across the road from the fire station. He had worked for Dennis in Guildford and came with the engine to Enfield. He and the well helmeted fireman behind him kept a careful eye on the shiny machine in this out of town ceremony.

Right: The locomotive and carriages had just arrived at Palmers Green Station on 26 October 1944. The steam was rising from the engine as it waited to continue on its journey. Passengers and the men on the footplate heard the drone of a long range rocket, the V2. Everybody tensed as its motor cut out. Seconds later there was a blinding flash and an almighty explosion. The track in front of the train was buckled and twisted. Debris flew everywhere. It

rained down on the carriages as bricks and roofing tiles were blown away from houses in the blast. Those on board the train were comparatively lucky. There was only one fatality. Most escaped unscathed. Others nearby were not so fortunate. Fifty-three people had to receive treatment for their injuries. The crater left by the V2 was 30 feet deep and 60 feet wide. Within two days this little army of railway workers had the hole filled in and the track relaid. Normal service was resumed. Residents had come to terms with being vulnerable. Earlier in the war it was thought that bombers would ignore Southgate's residential areas. There was little industry to be attacked. Edmonton was less secure. Children were evacuated from all of the industrial areas of East Enfield to safer retreats in the country. It soon dawned on the Southgate population that bombers did not have to miss by much to hit housing rather than factories. It was soon appreciated that the blitz on London in 1940-41 and the flying bombs of 1944-45 were not solely aimed at industry. Civilians had become fair game.

Above: Even though it was a cold day on 15 January 1932 the work had to go on. The construction workers' breath hung in the frosty air as they toiled away on the building of Southgate Viaduct. At this time the area looked more like a bomb site than part of an engineering feat. It all appeared haphazard, but looks are deceptive. There was a grand sense of order in the planning if not in the storage of the materials. From this apparent scene of chaos a great structure would ride. It eventually spanned the valley to the north of the station. The railway line carried on to Oakwood, the final stop before the Cockfosters terminus. At Oakwood a new suburb grew up around the station. Later, a new shopping centre on Bramley Road was developed near there. The Piccadilly Line originally ran from Hammersmith to Finsbury Park. By the 1920s the latter station and surrounding area had become very congested. Connections to trams, bus routes and the mainline railway meant that pressure built up to unmanageable proportions. Particularly at rush hour there was the 1920s' version of gridlock. By 1930 the work to extend the Tube to Cockfosters had been started. Splendid brick viaducts crossed Arnos Park and The Vale. New standards were set in engineering design. The extension to Arnos Grove was completed in 1932. Enfield West at Oakwood opened the following year.

Below: What a waste, as the late Ian Dury might have put it. There was certainly one blockhead who got his ear chewed by the boss after this crash in the 1960s near the junction of Hoppers Road and Stonard Road, Palmers Green, by the A111. The lorry driver had somehow managed to deposit most of his load of Skol lager on the pavement. There was glass and booze everywhere. Whoever caused this to happen was the original lager lout. The mopping up operation had just begun when the photographer arrived. A few people took the opportunity to stock up early for Christmas, but there was not much to be salvaged from the pavement. Most of the bottles that hit the flagstones were smashed on impact. Golden foaming liquid flowed into the drains. The rats in the sewers were staggering around for weeks afterwards. Anyone trying to smuggle a crate of lager away from the scene would have a difficult job hiding it under his jumper or persuading a policeman that he had just found it lying around. Drivers of drays and beer wagons were often given freebies each week. A few bottles of the brewery ale or distributor's product were part and parcel of their perks. The man behind the wheel of the Skol lorry did not dare to ask for his allowance. There would have been a danger of the foreman at the depot reaching for Ian Dury's rhythm stick. Reasons to be cheerful? Not for the poor chap responsible for this mess.

The firm with a golden touch

The name of Johnson Matthey is a familiar enough one in Enfield, and the company's metal refinery at Brimsdown is a well known local landmark. But with an annual group turnover approaching £4,000 million pounds and a presence in many countries throughout the world the Brimsdown site is just one part of a multi-national business with a history stretching back to the 18th century.

The story of Johnson, Matthey & Company can be conveniently divided into four periods:

The first from 1783 to 1817 which comprises the story of the Johnson business up to the time when Percival Norton Johnson started up in business for himself.

Secondly the period between 1817 and 1860 which is the story of P N Johnson and his partnership with George Stokes, W J Cock and George Matthey.

The third distinct period is from 1860 to 1914 during which years the modern business was built up by George Matthey, John Scudamore Sellon and Edward Matthey.

And lastly the period from 1914 leading to our present era.

The Johnsons were a London family living in Maiden Lane who during the eighteenth and nineteenth centuries founded their business of assaying bullion -

testing the purity of precious metals - and analysing useful minerals.

The first known member of the Johnson family was one Christopher Johnson a coachman who married in 1729 at the age of twenty-one at St Gregory's church in London.

Right: *Johnsons premises, Hatton Garden in the early 1930s.* **Below:** *A staff trip to Brighton in the early 1920s.*

7 Maiden Lane an address long associated with the family. In 1770 the Johnson mark was registered at the Goldsmiths' Hall consisting of the letters J J separated by an asterisk and surrounded by a rectangular frame.

By 1777 Johnson had taken up the profession of assaying that was to form the basis of his own and his descendants careers. In 1779 John Johnson took his fourteen year old son, also John, into the business as an apprentice. Seven years later, in the year his son was to complete his apprenticeship, John Johnson died.

Percival Johnson had been born in 1792 five years after John Johnson junior's marriage to his cousin Mary Wright. John Johnson's income for this period is preserved in the company archives as £337 during 1787, £439 in 1793 and £505 in 1795.

The work consisted of three parts. The first of these was the assaying of bullion by fire methods: melting, cupellation and 'parting' with nitric acid. The second consisted of dealing in bullion: buying scrap metal in the market, remelting, assaying and then selling it on to refiners. The third section was in pharmacy, retailing 'spirits of scurvy grass' rich in vitamin C and used to cure and prevent scurvy.

In 1751 the coachman's son John Johnson was apprenticed to one Richard Wright, a goldsmith, for seven years his father paying the sum of £21 for his son's education. By 1762 John Johnson had set himself up renting premises in New Prison Walk Clerkenwell as a jeweller. And subsequently number

A profitable development in the business came in the early years of the 19th century when Johnson began selling platinum exported from the Spanish colony of New Granada and arriving in England via Jamaica.

John Johnson junior retired at the age of fifty in 1817. John's elder son John Frederick had already been working for his father for some years as had his brother Percival who now managed the business and lived with his wife Elizabeth at Maiden Lane.

Above: Transporting materials in the early 1920s at Hatton Garden. Top: A bird's eye view of the Enfield site in the 1930s.

The London Directory for 1817 records Johnson P N Assayers of ores & metals 6 Maiden Lane, Wood Street with no mention of Percival's elder brother. According to tradition the two brothers had quarrelled and Percival the younger left, leading to their father's return to the business for another three years.

Percival set up on his own, assisted by £150 from his father. Percival did not however go very far, setting himself up in business at number 8 Maiden Lane before, in 1822, moving to 79 Hatton Garden where he sowed the real seeds of what would eventually become Johnson Matthey & Co Ltd.

The ideas on which Percival based his independent career were made up of a number of principles: the first was the need for greater accuracy and more precision in the assaying of bullion - at that time the degree of inaccuracy involved gave a useful if slightly dishonest margin for refiners to make a profit; to give greater confidence in his assaying Percival offered to buy back any bullion he had assayed. This led to his second principle that of becoming refiner of gold and silver. The third idea was to

Right: An aerial view of the site from 1949. **Below:** *Smelting ore in the 1930s.*

study and develop the uses of platinum which was just becoming more widely available and was attracting a great deal of interest in scientific circles.

Arising from the chemical handling of gold and the rise of the pottery and glass industries was the possibility of preparing a series of vitreous colours containing a portion of gold. The best known of those colours was the ancient preparation known as Purple of Cassius which consists of tin oxide impregnated to a deep purple colour by a very finely divided gold.

1851 and the Australian goldrush three years later.

Progress with platinum was not so rapid whilst the production of vitreous colours in those early years was best described as slow but steady, sales however consistently contributed to the firm's profits.

Johnson's interest in uranium ores led in turn to nickel and he established himself as the first refiner of nickel in Britain. An alloy with copper and zinc to produce nickel-silver meant the demand for nickel increased rapidly when that alloy became the base for silver-plating.

By 31 March 1860, when Percival Johnson retired, the business was well established in its five operating divisions and in that form would be passed on to his successors.

Mixed with other substances the preparation can provide a wide variety of pinks, mauves and purple of great value to potters and glass makers.

The accurate assaying of gold and silver was so successful that in 1852 the firm's reputation was to lead to its appointment as official assayers to the Bank of England.

In bullion refining Percival Johnson's crowning achievement was to succeed in refining the so-called 'complex bars' of metal from the Imperial Brazilian Mining Association containing tellurium and palladium which had defeated the best efforts of earlier refiners to separate. That triumph placed the firm at the head of the queue when it came to meeting the demands posed by the Californian goldrush of

Percival had no children of his own; although for a short while he had been in partnership with Thomas Cock and traded as Johnson & Cock between 1837 and 1845 that was now long past and new, young blood was needed.

That new blood came in the form of George Matthey. George was the son of Percival Johnson's stock-broker and he had entered the business as Johnson's apprentice in 1838.

Top: A staff celebration in the 1920s.
Above left: *Lord Robens speaking to Peter Ewing on a visit to Brimsdown in the early 1970s.*

Later Matthey's father invested the then enormous sum of £10,000 in the business. Matthey was to become known as a gifted scientist and a persistent and practical businessman.

By the beginning of 1850 Percival Johnson had laid out his plans for the future of the firm: John Scudamore Sellon, Johnson's nephew and Edward Matthey, George Matthey's younger brother, would become apprentices with the prospect of eventually becoming partners.

On 10 September 1851 Johnson took George Matthey into partnership and the firm became Johnson & Matthey.

Following Percival Johnson's retirement George Matthey, John Sellon and Edward Matthey became partners sharing profits one-half, one-third and one-sixth respectively; from that time on the firm would be known as Johnson, Matthey & Co.

George Matthey took to the side of the business which dealt with the application of chemistry whilst John Sellon turned to the commercial side and soon proved himself to be an able and far-sighted business man; something of a showman he developed a personal flair for seeking out new uses for precious metals; he was the real founder of the workshops which were to combine the application of platinum and precision engineering.

Edward Matthey having studied at the Royal School of Mines turned towards the metallurgical side of the business and supervised the rapidly growing bullion side of the firm, he was known as a steadying influence on his fellow directors and was seldom slow to remind them that it was his side of the firm which contributed the most to profits.

In 1891 the partnership was converted into a private limited company becoming, on 11th April of that year, Johnson Matthey & Company Ltd.

In the year of incorporation George Matthey the senior partner was 66 years old and although he continued as Chairman for another eighteen years until his death in 1909 he officially retired in 1902.
Edward Matthey was 55 in 1891 having devoted himself to furthering the interests of the business throughout his working life his main occupation having been to ensure

and maintain a solid foundation of paying business to serve as a sound basis for the more spectacular and speculative operations of his two partners.

Edward Matthey retired in 1904 but John Sellon continued in harness until 1918 after having been managing director since 1903 as well as becoming chairman following the death of George Matthey. In an interesting reflection of the times John Sellon's relatively long working life may be put down to the fact that, amongst the three directors, only he employed a secretary to help him!

A new generation was soon installed as directors, a generation which would see the firm through the rigours of the Great War of 1914-18.

Not all the next generation were a success: George Matthey's eldest son George a director until 1895 resigned apparently out of lack of interest. John Sellon's eldest son the delightfully named John Scudamore Pybus Sellon died during a sea voyage at the age of 36 in 1898.

One director who literally saw the firm through the Great War was Cyril Matthey, Edward Matthey's eldest son. Cyril Matthey joined the firm in 1885 aged 21 and seems to have been responsible for introducing accountancy to the business; he also took charge of the bullion department until 1914 when, despite his somewhat advanced age, he went to fight in France as Colonel of the London Rifle Brigade.

Top left: *21st century technology controlling production.* ***Top right:*** *Ladelling of silver anodes.* ***Above:*** *Removing silver from photographic film.*

The last of the junior directors was Percy Matthey, George's younger son who would in turn eventually become chairman from 1918 to 1928.

Interestingly for those who imagine directors doing no work the original articles of the company required the 'junior directors to be at work every day, including Saturdays from 9 am to 6 pm and to work all night if required.

In 1850 there had been fewer than twenty employees; by 1860, with increased work, that figure had doubled; by 1904 the number of employees had risen to 281 and by the outbreak of war in 1914 had exceeded 300.

Refining facilities had first been set up at Brimsdown in 1929 where demand for refined metals continued throughout the inter war year. Following the second world war these facilities were proving inadequate and work began on a new refinery completed in 1950 at a cost of £850,000 and capable of handling 200 tons of platinum ore a month. Yet in the longer term even that proved inadequate as the demand for platinum began to outstrip supply with further extensions being built in due course which would eventually evolve into the present site configuration.

No other company has been so deeply involved in the evolution of precious metals recovery as Johnson Matthey. The pioneers of highly modern techniques for mechanical sampling that are unrivalled in the industry. Johnson Matthey's refineries represent the world's most comprehensive and advanced refining facilities available.

The final product may be a metal, a chemical, a catalyst, or another fabri-cated product from the Johnson Matthey range, such as silver nitrate for the photographic industry. Alternatively, the customer may wish

to take advantage of Johnson Matthey's considerable expertise and standing in the world's metal markets to sell the metal on their behalf.

By 2000 the firm's turnover had reached an astonishing £3,866 million a year with annual profits of £143 million. As might be expected precious metals and colours and coatings provide many millions of those profits; perhaps however Percival Johnson the firms' founder would have been surprised to note that the largest component of those profits now comes from catalysts, chemicals and fuel cells. The continuing spread of vehicle emissions regulations around the world has pushed up global demand for Autocatalysts and Johnson Matthey is at the forefront of this technology; and in the World's search for more environmentally friendly vehicle fuel the development of the fuel cell has made great strides. The automotive industry is targeting to have the first "production" fuel cell vehicles on the road by 2005 and estimates that by 2010 1 million fuel cell cars will be produced. Johnson Matthey is playing a leading role in bringing this new and exciting technology to the market. Of course Percival Johnson would never have heard of the internal combustion engine nor have imagined the future need for catalytic converters containing platinum to control exhaust emissions. Nor could the founder have anticipated the uses to which precious metals are now put in the electronics and computer industries. Today the business is a world-wide enterprise with operations in USA, the UK, Belgium, Mexico, Argentina, South Africa, Malaysia, India, Sweden, Japan, Brazil, Germany, Canada, Hong Kong and the Netherlands - a long way from Maiden Lane.

Top left: *An aerial view of the site at the start of a new millennium.* ***Below:*** *Overseas customers visiting the firm in the early 1980s.*

Potions and pills at Ponders End

The pharmaceutical manufacturing plant of Merck & Co Inc at Enfield's Ponders End will be familiar to many local residents either under the MSD title or under the older name of Morsons. The plant has a long history.

In 1971 Thomas Morson & Son Ltd celebrated its 150th anniversary. When Thomas Morson (1799-1874) first opened his doors for business in 1821 - a full sixteen years before Queen Victoria ascended the throne - it was a small chemist's or apothecary's shop known simply as T Morson. Today the company is one of the most diversified and productive chemical manufacturers in the United Kingdom.

Morson has been part of MSD Ltd (a subsidiary of Merck & Co Inc) since 1957. On its nine acre site at Ponders End 'Morsons' manufactures a variety of chemical products including bulk chemicals for a number of human and animal health products marketed by MSDI. Most of the plant's output goes to Merck Sharp and Dohme Ltd at Hoddesdon for conversion into tablets, capsules injectables and other formulations, but Morson also supplies other Merck subsidiaries and customers in various parts of the world.

Right: *Milling operations, 1915.*
Below: *The yard in 1915.*

Thomas Morson's original establishment was located at 65 Fleet Market in the heart of London. Most of the medicines prepared in the shop were then derived from the bark, leaves, gums and resins of plants. Pills lozenges, solutions and ointments were made by hand along with toiletries and perfumes.

But the interests of the 22 year old proprietor Thomas Newborn Robert Morson went well beyond the mere formulating and dispensing of medicines.

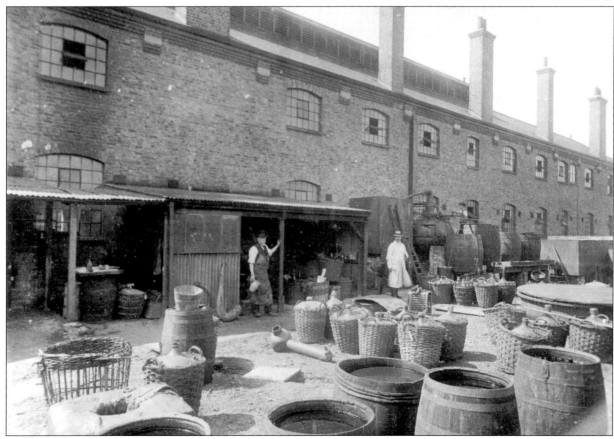

Antoine Lavoisier the great French chemist and Joseph Priestley in England had launched the modern age of chemistry in the last half of the 18th century with their studies of oxygen. New and far reaching advances followed, each firing the imagination of chemists all over Europe.

Following his marriage in 1822 to Charlotte Elizabeth Pegram - and a useful inheritance in 1824 when his father-in-law died - the firm moved to a new address, 19 Southampton Row in Bloomsbury. Price catalogues listed fine chemicals, patent medicines and the latest drug discoveries with 'their doses, so far as they are yet established'.

All manufacturing operations were transferred to the London suburb of Hornsey Rise in 1825. Here Morson worked out the first large-scale production of medicinal creosote and installed the first creosote stills - a product which was to enjoy major sales until 1940 when the war made exports impossible and allowed the American pharmaceutical industry to develop alternative supplies. By this time Thomas Morson had set up a private laboratory in his home to investigate new products and new processes.

Membership of the Royal Society of Arts and the Royal Institution of Great Britain brought Thomas Morson in constant contact with England's men of science. He was present at the meeting in the Crown and Anchor Tavern in Fleet Street in 1841 when plans were made to establish the Pharmaceutical Society of Great Britain (now the Royal Pharmaceutical Society).

Orphaned at an early age and thrown to a great extent on his own resources he was both practical and farsighted. Soon his apothecary workshop was expanding into the production activities which were to transform the small retail business into a large chemical manufacturing firm.

For a young man interested in chemical science the early decades of the 19th century were exciting times.

Top: The Boardroom pictured in August 1915, Thomas D Morson is seated right with his works manager left. **Left:** *The clerks office in 1915.*

He was vice president of the new Pharmaceutical Society in 1844, president in 1848 and a council member for 28 years. Thomas Morson was also a member of the distinguished Linnean Society a scientific organisation which is still active. He was personally acquainted with many famous scientists of his day including Michael Faraday famed for his experiments into the nature of electricity and Justus Von Leibig the father of agricultural chemistry.

The name T Morson & Son came into existence in 1854 when Morson created a partnership with his son Thomas junior.

In the mid 19th century Morson's major business had become the manufacture and supplying of extracts to the drug trade. Various raw materials were imported from France, Germany, China and Egypt. The finished products were exported to Australia, India, Canada and the United States as well as throughout Europe.

A popular product which was discovered and developed by Morson was a drug to aid digestion; derived from the stomach of pigs it was called Pepsine Porci.

A similar product had been invented in Germany some years earlier in 1846, that product, also made from pigs stomachs, was unpleasant though apparently not so bad as that made from sheep's stomachs by the French and was said to be utterly repulsive. Morson made a product which was pleasant - or at least not so unpleasant to take which produced relatively pure pepsin mixed with sago starch. The product became famous and continued to be manufactured until the 1920s sold in lozenges and globules. For those who were not so keen on pills to aid their digestion the firm also manufactured its own 'Pepsine' wine!

Top: Manufacturing potassium iodide, 1915.
Above: The eastern side of the factory looking south. Above left: Long service staff pictured together in 1923.

Morson also helped to advance the new field of photography with a collodion process which was used for many years.

A proud moment for T Morson & Son came when the company was awarded a medal for product excellence at the Great Exhibition of 1851 held in the Crystal Palace in London's Hyde Park.

On Thomas Morson's death in 1874 Thomas Morson junior inherited the business including the premises at Hornsey and Homerton. The pharmacy premises which were rented and renumbered from 19 to 124 in 1864 were compulsorily purchased by the Local Authority in 1900 to widen Southampton Row.

Thomas junior was 49 when he inherited the company and became the sole owner of a famed pharmacy and a pharmaceutical company with world wide interests. He was well qualified for the role having been educated at University College School and studying chemistry in Paris at the Institut Mathe and married the daughter of a French pharmacist.

At the time of the founder's death the turnover of the business was at least £30,000 a year with sales being to many of the country's largest hospitals as well as overseas including France, Germany, India and China.

Thomas junior decided to rationalise production and sold the Hornsey factory in 1875 to Edwards Ink Manufacturers for £2,500. All production then transferred to the other factory at Homerton. By the 1880s business was going well, sales had risen to £35,000 a year with profits of 25 per cent on turnover: Thomas and his son Thomas Pierre shared £4,000 between them in 1882, a very substantial sum when one recalls that experienced workers at that time received a mere £1.25 per week.

The firm's factory moved to Summerfield Works, Ponders End, Enfield in 1901, although until January 1957 the firm's head office would remain located at 47 Grays Inn Road in Holborn in London. The new offices at the works in Wharf Road were formally opened in June 1957 by the retired chairman Mr Leslie J Morson (1883-1974) great grandson of the founder, and Mr J Connor of Merck & Co with which Morson's had merged in February of that year.

Left: A staff photograph taken in 1936.
Below: Celebrations in the staff canteen in 1958.

At the ceremony Managing Director Geoffrey Morson, Leslie's son recalled that the firm had by then been a family business for 136 years.

Three acres were originally bought at Ponders End for a purchase price of exactly £1,000 the conveyance being completed on 8 May 1901. Prior to the arrival of Morsons the area of the Lea Valley in which Ponders End is situated was a district dominated by market gardening. The factory site had previously been allotments. Morsons' site was close to the railway which made travel to London easy and provided a siding from which goods could be easily transported.

In 1908 more land was bought taking the total to an archaic sounding 6 acres, 2 roods and 28 perches - or 6.68 acres.

Morsons spent some £20,000 buying the site and building their factory. All the equipment was transferred from Homerton including a 1,200 gallon chloroform still.

A house was provided on site for the manager including a garden planted with trees and shrubs. The first occupant of the house was one A J Tipping who had previously been works manger at Homerton. After A J Tipping's death in 1915 the house was converted to office use.

In 1898 aspirin was invented in Germany though little was produced in England until the outbreak of the first world war. Morsons undertook to provide the raw ingredients to British manufacturers and to act as selling agents, an arrangement which continued until as late as 1941.

The earliest link between the name of Morson and Merck seems to have been as long ago as 1930 when demand for a soluble calcium salt was increasing. The expert was E Merck of Darmstadt with whom discussions about a manufacturing and selling arrangement was soon initiated. After almost two years of negotiation the agreement was signed in July 1933. Merck & Co Inc agreed to provide their processes and a senior production chemist to demonstrate it; Morsons provided all the production facilities; profits were to be shared equally in an agreement intended to last for seven years. By 1939 more than 40,000lb of calcium glycerophosphate was being produced but the outbreak of war terminated the agreement and neither royalties, nor profits were paid or shared thereafter - somewhat ironic in the light of subsequent events.

The purchase of Morsons in 1957 by Merck & Co Inc in 1957 led to an immediate investment of half a million pounds which was used to reorganise and re-equip the factory which was soon producing two new diuretics, an antihyersenstive and an anti-rheumatic drug.

Top: *The Mayor and Mayoress of Enfield on a visit to the factory on July 3rd 1959.*
Above: *Mr L J Morson.*

Today Merck & Co Inc has four sites in the UK: Terlings Park in Essex is the company's research centre engaged in pioneering new treatments for diseases of the brain such as Alzheimer's disease, Parkinson's disease and stroke as well as migraine and pain. The firm's UK headquarters are at Hoddesdon in Hertfordshire where the sales, marketing, medical services, product development, market research and administration are based. Manufacturing is on two sites: a plant at Cramlington in

The origin of Merck & Co Inc can be traced back even further than Thomas Morson to an apothecary's shop on Darmstadt, Germany which was acquired by the Merck family more than 300 years ago. Today the company is a true multi-national with operations in over 200 countries and annual sales of over 32 thousand million dollars and more than 62 thousand employees.

Merck and Co Inc was originally an American off-shoot, set up in 1891, of the German firm of E Merck, itself established in 1827. Following sequestration of the American firm's stock in 1917 on the USA's entry into the Great War, George Merck was eventually able to buy back control of the firm at auction in 1919.

George W Merck, who became president of Merck & Co Inc in 1925, led the company to international prominence between the wars. Under the leadership of George Merck research became the company's driving force, his vision and influence paved the way for the isolation of vitamins B1, B6 and B12, the development of the first commercial synthetic corticosteroid - cortisone - and early bacterials and antibiotics such as the sulpha drugs, penicillin and streptomycin.

Two decisive mergers helped form the current company; the first in 1927 was with Powers Weightman Rosengarten which doubled the company's sales; the second, in 1953, with Philadelphia's Sharp and Dohme created today's internationally recognised name which would, over the coming years continue to expand and soon acquire Thomas Morson & Son.

Northumberland is one of the most advanced pharmaceutical packaging plants in the world. The bulk of chemical manufacture however remains at Ponders End. The Enfield factory is responsible for producing the active ingredients for some of the company's most important medicines; the active ingredient finasteride, used in the manufacture of prostate treatment, Proscar®, is made here and shipped world-wide. The Ponders End site has a distinguished record for safety and environmental concern and has been awarded the British Safety Council's 'Sword of Honour' no less than eleven times - the site's exemplary safety record is evident in its production record where no lost time has been recorded as a result of accidents for over 125 million working hours.

Today a permanent reminder of the origins of the Ponders End works remains in its address - Morson Road - named after its long gone founder Thomas Morson and the pharmaceutical business he established.

Above left: *Modern scientific machinery in 1991.*
Below: *An aerial view of the site taken in 1999.*

Lighting up Enfield

When the Atlas Fluorescent Tube Works in Enfield were completed on 25th October 1962, at a cost of two million pounds, the opening ceremony grabbed the attention of the whole nation - and not without good cause.

Today the factory belongs to one of the largest and most respected companies in the world, and one of the largest suppliers of light sources - the USA's GE Lighting - and so shares part of one of the most important chapters in global history.

In 1962 however the factory was still part of the Thorn Group. Chairman, managing director and founder Jules Thorn said that the Enfield site would prove to be one of the most important landmarks in the history of the company ranking alongside the production of his first Tungsten lamp in 1933.

For many years there had been a Thorn Atlas lamp available for every conceivable purpose, including traffic signals, signs and decoration, cycle dynamo lamps, aircraft and airfield floodlighting, cars, buses, trains, yachts and coach lamps.

Thorn had opened his first high-speed production plant at Enfield in 1948 for the mass production of tubular lamps. The company was already producing millions of incandescent electric lamps at other Thorn sites at Edmonton, Tottenham, Preston and Merthyr Tydfil and was responsible for almost fifty per cent of the country's fluorescent tube exports.

GE Lighting, which bought the factory in 1991, is a direct descendent of the General Electric Company formed by Thomas Edison in 1892, the company has become a major force in Europe through its direct investments, strategic alliances, joint ventures and partnerships.

The electric lamps made today have come a long way from a fateful meeting of the Newcastle Literary and Philosophical Society, on 3rd February 1879, when its 700 members watched Joseph Swan give the first demonstration of an 'electric incandescent vacuum lamp', which came to be known as 'the flameless light'. Few members could have doubted they had just witnessed history in the making. That same year Thomas Edison in the USA developed his own version of the flameless light.

Swan did not think the invention needed a patent, but Thomas Edison patented his own version which he called the 'electric lightbulb'; the two joined forces in 1883, forming the Edison and Swan

This page: *Joseph Swan.*

United Electric Light Company. For many years the Thorn company in Britain continued to use the brand name of 'Ediswan' for their lamps commemorating the historic partnership between the two scientists.

The Thorn Lighting company was started by Jules Thorn on 28th March 1928, as the Electric Lamp Service Co Ltd. Its success over a sixty years' history remains unrivalled. From meagre beginnings as a small lampworks, it eventually grew to Thorn Lighting, a large international company, with a zest for both customer satisfaction and technological advancements in lights and light-fittings.

Thorn began selling filament lamps at below the normal prices. Thorn always attempted to undercut his rivals - giving the same quality product and service but at a more affordable price.

The average selling price of tungsten lamps was then about five shillings each and, despite financial advice to the contrary, Thorn set up his own business. It was seen at the time as a major risk. In 1932 the supply of raw materials almost all but dried up, and yet Thorn took a gamble on buying premises in Angel Road, in Edmonton, North London and described in hindsight as a rather rough-and-tumble affair, originally called the Atlas lampworks.

But the gamble paid off. Just four years later, the business had won sufficient confidence from the public to form a public company to be floated on the stock market. There was a rush by subscribers to buy the five-shilling shares and the offers were oversubscribed 36 times. The company then rented its head office premises on Judd Street, a building owned and rented from the Salvation Army in Central London.

'Thorns' invested in a second factory site at Tottenham, during the Second World War, just in case the original plant at Edmonton had got destroyed during the Blitz - Luckily, it didn't.

Above left: *Jules Thorn - who established the Electric Lamp Service Company.* ***Top:*** *A window display from 1915.*

By the early 1940 s, creating fluorescent strip lighting was still a skilled craft which involved a worker blowing air into the hot glass which created the strip bulb. The mass production of such tubular fluorescent strip lamps was first introduced by Thorn following the end of World War Two when it opened a high-speed plant in 1948 in Enfield. Horizontal production machines arrived in 1962.

In 1950, 'Thorns' bought the majority of shares in the lighting manufacturing division of the Ekco-Ensign Electric Company Ltd, and purchased the remainder of the company sixteen years later. In the following six years, Thorn equipped it's ever-increasing number of factories with the best machinery available to produce the finest incandescent lighting in Europe. This period also marked ventures overseas for Thorn Industries, as its business began to extend throughout the western world.

In 1951, the introduction of 'double-life tubes' into the 'Atlas' range of lamps, enabled Thorn to offer its customers a guaranteed average effective life of 5,000 hours of their products.

Thorn House, at the time one of London's tallest and most modern buildings, opened on 7th September 1959 as Head Office for Thorn's subsidiary company, Atlas Lighting.

The first two years of the 1960s saw Thorn's innovations reach new peaks: the quartz-iodine lamp, known by most people as the tungsten halogen lamp was introduced in 1961, and proved to be one of the greatest advancements ever in lamp technology.

The very next year, a collaboration between Thorn and the Royal Aircraft Establishment produced the VASI system - the Visual Approach Slope Indicator for aircraft landings and further proved to be a substantial achievement in aviation safety - it's effects have revolutionised air systems and modern updated systems are based on the ideas of that early Thorn innovation.

Many famous events and venues were lit by the lamps produced by the Thorn empire: The flood-lighting of the first televised match in colour by Thames TV was Wolves v Spurs in 1969; the constantly-changing coloured illuminations at the Brighton Pavilion; the prize-winning floodlighting scheme amid the ruins of Coventry Cathedral in 1972; CEGB's Dinorwic pumping storage station at Llanberis was floodlit with spectacular lights in 1979; Muhammed Ali's title-winning fight against Joe Bugner in 1975, in Kuala Lumpur, was backed by CSI floodlights; the vast Vicente Caldero stadium in Madrid; lighting at the

Above: *Early advertisements for Mazda lightbulbs.*
Top: *The company staff in 1934.*

Sydney Opera House and the ice arenas for the Winter Olympic games; Thorn Lighting won three of the four categories of the industry's top Lighting Federation Awards in 1987, for lighting the Newport Leisure Centre.

By 1988, three years before its sale to General Electric's GE Lighting, Thorn Lighting could claim to be the largest producer of light fittings in the world outside of the USA and Japan.

Committed to commitment, excellence, innovation and quality, GE Lighting (Europe division) has invested more than $750 million in Europe in recent years and is the largest supplier of light sources in the world. Manufacturing facilities exist in the UK, Italy,

Germany and Hungary along with six major distribution centres around Europe.

Customers have the benefit of GE Lighting's expertise gained through the range of other skills and services it offers within the industries catered for by the company - its policies and practices have been adopted by other major companies throughout the world. The success of the GE company not only came from Swan's discovery and Edison's subsequent inventions - it has also been a pioneer and forerunner in the field of electric-power for many years, and in many different ways. Whilst these other ventures enabled the General Electric Company to branch out into the manufacture of aircraft engines to a whole range of systems for the industrial, medical, satellite, information and information technology sectors, it is the electric light and its whole range of applications which has remained the focus of GE Lighting.

In 1907 GE Lighting was the first company to use Tungsten which improved on the earlier carbon-based filaments. It proved to be both twice as efficient and twice as long-lasting as the earlier components - and further improvements were made. The company is still making advances in the use and application of Tungsten to make greater value for customers.

Greater durability and vibration-resistance multiplied the uses and applications of the tungsten lamp- and it was eventually sold into other areas catering for industrial, commercial and transport sectors.
The next time you watch a soccer match, remember

Left: *The filament mounting department in Enfield c1949.* **Below:** *Blowing the glass tubing for fluorescent lamps in the late 1930s.*

that GE Lighting originally developed the mercury vapour technology which made the first practical sports stadium and good outdoor street lighting possible.

In 1958 GE Lighting was also responsible for inventing the halogen lamp, the bright, white lighting often used to illuminate public spaces, homes and offices.

And what of fluorescent strip lights which has transformed millions of offices, factory and domestic premises world-wide? In 1938, on the threshold of the second world war, GE Lighting was also the first company to produce fluorescent lighting which, again, marked a major change in the way our lives were lived.

All pioneering companies are committed to further developing their products which further enhance the quality of peoples lives, GE are constantly branching out into new directions. Fancy a change of career? GE and its subsidiary companies have led the way in innovative management techniques - so successful that they have been adopted by other companies. The company employs over 290,000 people world-wide, where everyone is given the opportunity to organise his or her own career development. It promotes a healthy business environment where everyone matters and ideas for commercial growth are invited from all quarters.

Their ideas are limitless and involve everyone in this constantly changing business environment - open to ideas from anywhere, seeing change not as an impending threat but as an opportunity for success and advancement.

Despite owning businesses such as GE Lighting, the General Electrical Company is probably best known for its ownership of NBC, the US television network. Responsible for such programmes as 'Frasier' and 'The Tonight show with Jay Leno'. The period of 1997-1998 saw NBC as the most watched TV network in the whole of America - for the third time in a row.

While being committed to commercial excellence in business, the GE group has helped many different organisations and individuals, in an extensive range of activities. GE created Elfun - which is a world-wide group of volunteers, mainly retired GE employees, who work to help the less fortunate become more independent and therefore lead a better quality of life. The visually impaired have

Above: Ekco -Ensign Electric was taken over by Thorn in 1950. Below: One of the fluorescent tube production units in the 1950s.

students whilst other schemes are aimed at helping the homeless and rebuilding and repairing zoos and other nature and wildlife parks throughout the world.

Within the GE group GE Lighting has gone from strength to strength, it is continually looking to break the boundaries within which other businesses unwittingly limit themselves; the company's place in the history of Enfield is certainly assured. Having encouraged the area to prosper and boom from their first appearance in the town, creating and maintaining much needed employment for local people, the company will no doubt continue to command respect from the local community for many years to come.

benefited from Elfun's work to build more than 22,000 talking book machines which act as tools for the visually impaired to boost their lives in both educational and entertaining ways.

The global company also provided the funding for a Chinese version of the children's learning programme 'Sesame Street', to reflect Chinese culture and help the nation's children prepare for school in an entertaining way.

Tutoring at a Distance is a special programme aimed at increasing literacy through computers, for people throughout the world. Projects initiated by GE help many sections of the community including

Above: *Fluorescent tubes used to display the Hillman Minx at the 1951 Earls Court Motor Show.* **Top:** *Thorn in the 1960s.* **Right:** *An aerial view of the premises today.*

A credit to Enfield

How on Earth did previous generations manage without hire purchase and credit cards?

It is difficult now for the young to imagine that only a few decades ago credit shopping was a very different proposition than it is today. Certainly some sectors had well developed credit schemes, buying clothes on tick from the talleyman was a common enough experience for the less well off, as well as putting it 'on the slate' at the corner shop or pub.

Having 'an account' was however something that only the better off were familiar with. Even then the system of credit offered by suppliers was a purely personal one with hand written accounts periodically delivered to customers who were personally known to the tradesmen involved.

Such arrangements had existed both formally and informally for generation upon generation and, in their own small way, contributed to smoothing the economic wheels of the whole national economy and, in a smaller way, to the household economies of individuals and their families.

Not that everyone bought goods on credit; indeed in some quarters the very idea of being in debt was frowned upon. In many households, even some of the poorest,

*Above: Jules Thorn who founded his own hire purchase business which was to become the Retail Finance Division of First National. **Right:** Head office in the 1970s.*

the very idea of being in debt was viewed with absolute horror: folks' memories of the poorhouse and tales of the debtors prisons of the 19th century persisted in the nation's minds long after the last of them had closed. The maxim 'if you can't afford it, do without it' was a popular saying repeated endlessly by parents desperate to ensure that they and their children stayed on the straight and narrow.

In the 1950s however things began to change. The austerity of the economic depression of the 1930s and rationing during the second world war were past and economic recovery was on its way. By the end of the decade Harold Macmillan would be telling voters that they had never had it so good. And it was true. Employment levels had never been higher and men and women were boasting that they could walk out of a job at lunchtime and have another, better paid one an hour later. But where did that new found prosperity come from? Part of the answer certainly lay in consumer credit and the public's attitude to it.

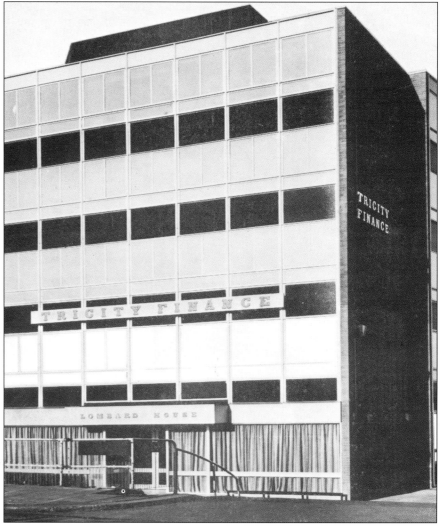

In the midst of the 1950s' economic boom one factor which was slowing down production and keeping demand in check was customers inability to pay cash for goods. This was especially true of the new consumer goods then becoming widely available in Britain for the first time but which we now take for granted: fridges, cookers, televisions and record players. Such goods were expensive but for the first time were coming within the reach of the ordinary working man and woman.

One man in particular who had cause for concern was Jules Thorn the founder of the Thorn electrical company who reasoned that if some way could be found to provide credit to potential customers even more of the products from the Thorn factories would be sold. He would establish his own hire purchase business. The idea was a stroke of genius, delivering the right product at exactly the right time. Not only were such financial services viable and safe in a growing economy but for the first time many of the public who had been unhappy to buy 'on tick' felt able to do so. That change of heart had little to do with any moral opposition to debt but rather the removal of the fear of its consequences. For the first time in thirty years most members of the public felt confident that they would have jobs for long enough to pay off any debt they incurred and, perhaps more importantly, the Welfare State, which had been inaugurated in July 1948, would act as a safety net preventing them from falling into penury should they lose their jobs.

> *In the 1950s the austerity of the 1930s depression and wartime rationing was over and economic recovery was on its way*

Jules Thorn's brainchild was born at the perfect moment in history and would eventually evolve into today's First National Retail Finance Division, one of Enfield's most prominent companies with a turnover measured in hundreds of millions of pounds each year and financing up to ten thousand transactions a day.

Today no other finance house in the country offers a range of credit plans with the same refinement as First National and that, combined with the knowledge and expertise built up by the company, has enabled it to become the leader in the retail point-of-sale finance sector.

Left: *Early computers in the Creditcharge department.* **Below:** *The Call Centre in the 1980s.*

In the aftermath of the second world war however money was tight and credit to enable people to buy goods whilst spreading payments over an affordable time period was seldom easily available. The company was originally incorporated on 31st January 1955 as the Tricity Finance Corporation Limited and actually commenced operations in the back of a garage in Eaton Road, Enfield where it undertook 'stocking finance' for retailers and credit facilities for individual customers. Business continued in a shed by the Ferguson building known locally as the Elephant House located on the corner of Southbury Road and Great Cambridge Road - where the closed Safeway store now is.

The business was well supported by retailers who welcomed being able to offer credit facilities in respect of Thorn merchandise such as Tricity cookers and fridges. On 6th November 1959 Lombard Banking Limited, as it was then known, purchased a majority 51 per cent share holding in the company leaving Thorn Electrical Industries with 49 per cent; that relationship continued until August 1980 when Lombard North Central PLC purchased the remainder of the Thorn shares providing funds for the Thorn Group to purchase EMI.

Lombard North Central, the firm's parent company, celebrated a unique achievement in the finance world during February 1986. With an enviable record of success, in that year it had been in business for 125 years thus making it the oldest finance house in Great Britain.

In the years immediately following its formation however Tricity Finance occupied a number of buildings within the Borough of Enfield including Cecil Court, Refuge House, offices in Baird Road, Burleigh House and New River House.

None of those premises were ever entirely suitable for their purpose. The building at Baird Road for example had been designed for a small engineering company not as an office; it had a glass roof and in summer it got so hot that free ice-creams were handed out to staff and men were allowed to remove their ties; when the heating broke down in winter the management went round handing out hot soup.

The company moved to Tricity House, Southbury Road, Enfield in May 1961, a building which was

*Above: Point of Sale material. **Below:** The New Business department.*

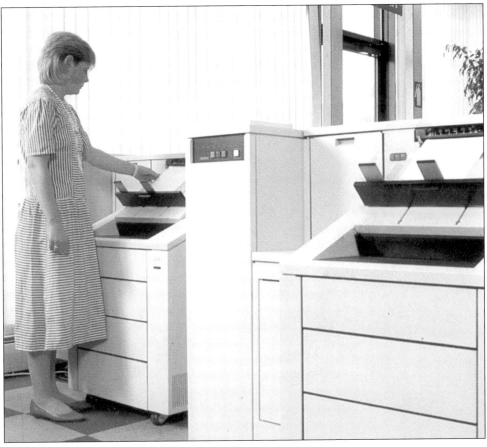

publicity point of view, the company's name was changed to Lombard Tricity Finance Limited on 1st January 1982. The company moved its head office again, this time to Baird Road, Enfield, over the August Bank Holiday weekend in 1982. Apparently never keen to stay in one place too long the company however returned to its present head office at Tricity House in July 1991.

Britain in the 1980s was undoubtedly becoming a credit card country. Before the end of the decade more than 32 million people

purpose built for the firm's use by the Thorn Group. Over the next few years the firm continued to seek new business and diversified into larger unit finance such as vending machines, office/commercial furniture, furnishings and car wash equipment. That finance was handled on both a Direct and Block Discount basis.

In January 1968 the company's policy was changed to concentrating on the consumer durable market from which point the company has gone from strength to strength, one of the first successful large negotiations having been the purchase of the existing accounts from the Electrolux subsidiary Beechwood Finance Limited and the under-taking of all other new finance for Electrolux merchandise. This duly had the effect of doubling the size of Tricity which eventually led to the purchase of the old Lombard House at 286 Southbury Road Enfield in 1968. In that same year, 1968, the company also changed its name to the slightly shorter Tricity Finance Ltd.

Because of the much closer relationship and the benefits to be gained from an advertising and

would hold credit or charge cards of one kind or another - with over 10 million store cards believed to be in circulation nation-wide.

The dramatic rise in the number of store cards reflected overall changes in marketing strategy within the High Street as financial services became entwined with retail business

By the end of 1985 the amount of retail credit outstanding in the personal sector had reached a staggering 65 per cent of income compared to only 25 per cent at the beginning of the decade - and there was nothing to suggest that that proportion might not continue to rise.

Stores began to promote credit as an added benefit to encourage customer loyalty. The success of the personalised store card was fuelled by the philosophy of offering credit to retail customers to improve their lifestyle immediately rather than having to wait for credit approval.

Above: The Index and Enquiries section.
Top: Computer hardware in the 1980s.

Providing credit is not however a risk free business. The collapse of furniture retailer Maples at the end of 1997 plunged Tricity £10 million into the red creating a real threat of closure. The company implemented a recovery programme which resulted in turning that anticipated massive loss into an end-of-year profit of £5 million! Not surprisingly Strategic Risk Management is now one of the company's core areas of expertise.

In 1999 the First National Bank purchased Tricity together with two other Lombard companies. The firm's name was changed yet again - this time to First National Tricity Finance Ltd (FNTF) forming the Retail Finance Division of the First National Group.

The decision by Natwest, owners of the Lombard Group, to focus on dealing directly with personal and business customers, offered First National Bank the chance to rapidly advance its expansion plans. Convinced by, and committed to the future of the intermediary marketplace, FNB Managing Director Philip George described the company as the 'jewel in the Lombard crown'.

Today the company operates in three core markets - home furnishings, electrical goods and personal

computers supplying finance to eight of the top thirteen retailers in the firm's chosen market and have over 300 retailer clients including DFS, Furnitureland and Harveys in home furnishings; Dixons, ScottishPower and Powerhouse in electrical goods and Tiny Computers, Time Computers and Mesh Computers in PCs each having the facility to offer point of sale finance such as interest free credit, budget accounts, deferred credit, payment protection and store cards.

Top: *The highly popular annual Gala Day, organised by the Sports and Social club.*
Above right: *A merchandiser in the showroom.*
Right: *A view of the open plan office.*

In 2000 the company entered a strategic partnership with Experian, the global information company, to deliver state of the art customer relation management solutions. That partnership, incorporated as FN Services Ltd, allows the firm to capitalise on its operational developments whilst enabling it to focus on developing value-added activities.

Originally all finance proposals were sent by post for processing. In the early 1970s Tricity invested in the technology to handle proposals by telephone and opened for business on a Saturday for the first time. On that first Saturday the firm received just seven telephone calls; today Tricity operates seven days a week and takes over 10,000 calls on Saturdays alone.

The company is now focusing on building on the First National brand and its mission statement is 'to build a winning business with leading partners to drive the retail finance market'. For nearly half a century they have been providing finance to enable consumers to buy goods on credit. The services provided by Jules Thorn's baby have enabled millions of people to buy goods they might otherwise have never been able to buy and enabled tens of thousands of retailers to sell goods they might have otherwise been unable to sell.

The scale of the enterprise today is breathtaking and computers have long since displaced the early comptometers and paper. Surely however even a man as visionary as Jules Thorn would have been astonished to see how far his finance company has come since its incorporation in 1955. And we would guess he would be equally astonished to see, at the beginning of the third millennium, how credit, once thought of as unusual, is now one of the most common ways of buying goods - with some claiming that the day is not far off when a customer paying with cash will be as rare a sight as a penny farthing bicycle.

Left: *Members of the Sales Team at an exhibition.*
Below: *A recent view of the Head Office.*

The Wright mix of the finest ingredients

During the 17th, 18th and 19th centuries, three events took place which were to make a tremendous difference to our national enjoyment of bread. In the mid-17th century Ponders End Mill was constructed; around a hundred years later the 4th Earl of Sandwich first ate meat between slices of bread and invented the sarnie; and another hundred years or so after that, the Wright family started milling at Ponders End Mill.

When the mill was built in around 1650, it was called not Ponders End but Flanders Mill, and it had seven pairs of millstones driven by two water wheels. It replaced an earlier mill, and in fact a mill is believed to have occupied the site ever since 1067. In the 18th century Flanders Mill was re-named Enfield Mill, and by the time George Reynolds Wright arrived, the name had been changed again, to Ponders End.

George Reynolds Wright was a farmer's son from Hitchin who had decided to make his own way in the world. He became a miller's apprentice and gradually wove his way south, moving first to Luton, then to Welwyn and finally to Enfield, where he went into partnership with another miller, James Dilly Young.

Young & Wright, the new owners of Ponders End, began a new era in the long history of the mill when they started production, milling around 1,000 tonnes of flour a year.

Following the death of James Young, George Reynolds Wright carried on the business under his own name. In 1880 the mill was extended and partially rebuilt, another five pairs of millstones were added, and a steam engine was installed to drive them. G R Wright was determined that only flour milled from the finest ingredients should bear his name, and his business was clearly thriving. In due course George's three sons began to learn the trade. George William, the eldest, was killed in a tragic accident in 1896, but Walter and Leonard both stayed with their father. When George Reynolds reached the age of 60 and began to think of retiring, he decided to turn the mill into a limited liability company under the direction of himself and his two sons. G R Wright and Sons Limited was formed in 1913, with Walter James Wright as Chairman, and the founder began to spend less time at the mill and more time pursuing his local interests and serving the local community as councillor and JP.

By the time the second generation took over, considerable advances had taken place at the mill. A steam wagon costing £496 had been purchased on 31st August, 1906, and this was capable of transporting loads far heavier than the 40 sacks, or 5 tons, that the horse-drawn wagon had been able to carry.

Above: *George Reynolds Wright, JP, company founder.* ***Below:*** *The mill staff in 1912.*

A continental roller mill system had been intro-duced - although millstones were still used to grind Wright's special Imperial Wholemeal. The mill had been converted to electricity, supplied by the Enfield Electricity Company. Extra wheat bin accommodation had been erected; and a new 12-sack mill was being planned. However, the family's plans were brought to an abrupt halt when war broke out and the Government took control of the country's flour mills. This situation lasted until 1920, when finally the mills were decontrolled, in a climate of severe economic depression, and competition became so intense that many were driven out of business. Ponders End Mill - with Leonard's son George William, the sole representative of the third generation of the family, now taking an interest - not only survived the inter-war years but continued to invest for the future. A 90 feet high silo was constructed, improving the efficiency of the business; and the company had just purchased the freehold of the 11-acre site from the Metropolitan Water Board, for the sum of £6,000, when war broke out again.

This picture: *Wheat arriving by barge in 1955.*

Again the mill was brought under government control. Bomb damage to the mills in the London Docks meant that Ponders End Mills had to maintain production 7 days a week, 52 weeks a year, and this naturally took its toll on the plant and machinery. The mill escaped any direct hits, although on one occasion a German bomber was shot down overhead and the front of the building was sprayed with stray bullets. The bomber ended up in the Ponders End sewage works.

When life returned to normal again after the second world war, the company's first concern was to replace the plant, which required renewing having worked endlessly through the war years. This was not possible for some years, but in 1950 Thomas Robinson of Rochdale was called in, work was halted for around ten weeks, and when the mill re-started it had 50 per cent greater capacity and was capable of producing more than a dozen 280 lb sacks an hour. Later that same decade a new pre-cast concrete silo was erected, bringing total storage capacity up to 1,400 tons, and in 1960 an extension to the existing roller-mill was begun. This was completed the following year and further increased the plant's capacity by around 60 per cent.

All these improvements were made during the time that George William Wright was managing director. His only son, Kenneth Reynolds Wright, had come into the firm briefly after the war, but had then emigrated to Southern

Rhodesia in order to run a smallholding with his brother-in-law. In 1963 George William Wright died, and Kenneth returned to take over as MD. Under his leadership many more changes took place: sophisticated storage and packing systems were installed, a comprehensive fleet of modern vehicles was built up, storage capacity was increased, and two new plants were added.

Above: Adjusting the rolls, 1953.
Above left: Kenneth Reynolds Wright.
Top: The mill circa 1960.

domestic bread baking machines has reawakened interest in home baking, and Wright's bread mixes are an ideal way for people to enjoy delicious speciality breads straight from their own oven. Their mixes received such an enthusiastic response from the public that three years ago the company launched Wright's Home Baking Club. Already thousands of people have joined the club; membership is free, and members receive regular product updates and recipe ideas. Readers who would like to discover the pleasures of baking their own bread are cordially invited to telephone the club's freephone number, 0800 064 0100, for more information and a free recipe book.

There was a significant shift in the pattern of manufacturing, and retailing during the 1950s and 60s, with a general trend towards doing things on a larger scale. Mass-produced goods dominated the marketplace, and large supermarkets began to replace the corner shop. This trend affected the baking industry, with large plant bakeries growing up and threatening to drive the family baker out of business. G R Wright & Sons adapted to the new markets, without compromising the principles upon which the business was founded - to use only the finest ingredients and top quality wheats. The new supermarkets and later the growing number of Asian cash-and-carry stores became customers for Wright's range of bulk or bagged flour, along with the traditional craft bakeries. Today, G R Wright delivers to the major multi-outlet retailers such as Greggs, Sainsbury's, Tesco, Waitrose and also to customers in Norway, France, Holland, the Lebanon and the Carribean.

With the small craft bakeries in mind, G R Wright went on to develop a range of bread mixes which would allow craft bakers to bake high quality speciality breads such as Sundried Tomato, Sunflower, Sussex Nutty, Lemon & Ginger and Sticky Malt, without having to stock the dozens of ingredients needed to make them from scratch. These are also widely used by in-store bakeries, and new varieties continue to be added; Ciabatta, Naan and Chilli have been introduced over the last few years and are proving very popular. In recent years, the availability of

Today, G R Wright & Sons is London's only independent, privately owned, family run mill, and is run by David Wright, son of Kenneth Reynolds Wright and a direct descendant of the founder. The company mills as much flour in a week as once it did in a year, and work is currently under way on a £2million warehouse packing and storage facility, visible from Meridian Way. When complete, this will be the most modern and sophisticated of its kind in Europe. Enfield's oldest company is leading the industry in the 21st century: it was the first mill to achieve accreditation to BS EN ISO 9002, it has achieved Investors in People status, and it was the first company in the UK to develop a non-genetically modified alternative to soya based products used in bread baking. Ponders End Mill has tradition to be proud of. The company attributes its success to its commitment, first-class quality and service - not forgetting the loyal service of its staff, many of whom have worked there for more than 40 years. Above all, George Reynolds Wright's principles have never been forgotten. The mill has expanded, modern manufacturing and distribution systems have been introduced, the latest product testing and development techniques are used, and the product range has diversified considerably - but one thing that never has changed, and never will, is the assurance that everything that bears GR Wright's name has been made from only the finest ingredients.

*Top: Wright's successful range of speciality bread mixes. **Above left:** James Wright demonstrates how easy it is to make bread. **Right:** David Wright, Managing Director.*

Putting the colour into the automotive industry

In 1957 'Slim' Moring founded Morelli & Co, on the hunch that he could provide a better service to the motor repair trade than he could get for his own repair shop Moring & Co. The name came from Slim's early partnership with Mr Bert Ellis, Moring and Ellis being chopped together to form the Italian sounding Morelli.

Previously Slim worked as General Manager for Harold Radford at Harold Radford Ltd a coachbuilder making bespoke bodies to go on Bentley chassis. The Bentley Countryman sold to discerning English country gentlemen who needed lots of room for luggage for those weekends in the country.

However it was perhaps only inevitable that Slim would strike out on his own with a car repair garage as Moring & Co, at the garages behind 39 High Street, Southgate in 1953. But after a few years he was becoming very dissatisfied with his only source of supply for the repair products which he used. In those days there was only one supplier and you received a once or twice a week delivery service.

A premises was available at 39 High Street, Southgate, below the flat where Slim and his wife Win lived with their children David, Joan, John and soon to be born Ruth. All that was needed was a paint product to supply the trade, and Valentine Paints put their faith in Slim, supporting him with six months credit and a loan of £1,000. From day one Slim wanted to provide daily delivery service and decided to take on a large amount of stock so that back orders were a rarity.

Above: Founder C J 'Slim' Moring and his wife Win.
Right: The original premises, 39 High Street, Southgate.

So on the 27th May 1957 Morelli & Co opened their doors to the motor trade, the first day was not a great success. The first customer was the landlord who ran the pub opposite the shop who spent 7s. 2d. on a 2lb tin of paint. The ten shilling note that he used never made it to the bank and still takes pride of place on the Morelli Head Office wall today.

Slim's aim was £100 per month within the first six months, his first months takings topped £160 the second month £400 and in the third month £600 which then doubled in the fourth month. It seemed that Slim's hunch that he could do a better job than other suppliers was paying off. This is something that The Morelli Group, as the company is known today still believe strongly.

Morelli & Co formed a close working relationship with Valentine Paints and secured sole trading rights for the products for the North London and Essex areas. The early slogan for Slim Moring's car repair business was 'your stock is at the end of the telephone' and this was to remain the slogan for many years.

Slim ran the business while Win provided much needed administrative support, with clerical work and answering the telephones - not to mention supplying Slim with endless cups of tea and bacon butties! Their delivery vans were painted in a distinctive two tone green on top and black on the bottom half with gold lettering making them very distinctive to local people and customers alike.

The company soon expanded, with branches at Uxbridge, Ilford, Camden and Chelmsford but Southgate remained the Head Office with seven staff. By the 1970s there was a need for expansion at Southgate, Slim and Win had moved out of the flat above the shop but more space was needed for clerical staff and the increased stocks that the company was carrying. 100 yards down the road at 75 High Street, Southgate was a corner plot with a house next door, this was chosen as the new Morelli Head Office.

After considerable redevelopment the new shop, warehouse and office was opened for business. This site was to remain the Head Office until 1998 by which time it had been extended from 65-75 High Street.

The 70s saw a boom in car customising with special paint effects, flames, furry trim and airbrush murals being top of the agenda. Special paints from the USA became very fashionable and to promote these products Morelli had a Renault 4 delivery van customised.

Left: C J Moring pictured at the International Motor Show, Earls Court, London in 1952 whilst he still worked for Harold Radford (Coachbuilders) Ltd.
Top: A Mark II 'Countryman' Saloon on Harold Radford's stand at the 1952 motor show.

The murals were airbrushed by the same man who appeared on Blue Peter and did a portrait of the dogs, showing off his airbrush skills to the nation's children. The Custom Car show at Alexandra Palace was an

essential diary date and sales came from retail and trade customer alike.

Slim was by now pursuing a lifelong dream and was restoring Rolls Royce cars as a hobby using his years in the motor repair trade and product knowledge gained from his Valentine Agency with some superb results. He even restored a Bentley Countryman, the car he had helped design many years previously.

The 80s saw a push toward the trade customer and new paint products were introduced to facilitate this as the Valentine Brand began to loose it's place in the market. German cars were very popular and a German paint brand Glasurit was taken on to help sales in these areas. North London was thriving and Southgate was proving a good location with its access to the surrounding area and Hertfordshire playing an important part in the company's growth.

Morelli & Co became The Morelli Group and the company expanded out as far as Norwich and High Wycombe with 13 branches in total. Sadly Slim passed away in 1984 at the age of 67. By now The Board of Directors was made up of Slim's wife Win and his sons David and John as well as Joan's husband Colin Laybourn and John's brother in-law Allan Toms.

Centre: 71-75 High Street, Southgate before development. It was the Morelli Group Head Office for more than 20 years. **Above:** *Ruth Moring and the Morelli & Co custom van.* **Top:** *The Morelli stand at The Custom Car Show, Alexandra Palace.*

But, despite its success, the Morelli Group have never forgotten what made the company successful in the first place and its mission statement is still the same as ever. The quality of the service offered to customers remains of paramount importance to Morelli and probably explains the success of the company more than any other single factor.

The Southgate Head Office grew to include the three shops that were in the same parade of shops beside the house, with around ten clerical staff and fifteen shop/warehouse staff. But as the 90s went by it became obvious that more room was needed. The importance of the high street location had diminished as the focus on the trade customer heightened, so a new premises was found in Baird Road, Enfield.

Whilst the Enfield premises was being developed in 1998, the Morelli Group sponsored the British Expedition to Mount Everest which reached the summit at 7:30am 26th May 1998. From humble beginnings in Southgate to Everest and the top of the world in just over 40 years Slim would have been very proud.

Morelli's presence in Southgate came to an end after over 40 years when Enfield opened it's doors for trading in 1998, 7,000 sq. ft. at Southgate was replaced by 18,000 sq. ft. at Enfield. The Enfield premises has some 15 clerical staff and 25 shop and warehouse staff. The customer base now includes bodyshops and mechanical shops, but also includes woodfinish customers and other paint related industries such as engineering, manufacturing and modelmakers.

The Group employs over 175 staff and turns over in excess of £20 million there are now 10 strategically positioned branches in London and the Home Counties, with the latest purpose built industrial unit being built in Wickford, Essex.

Product is no longer just sold to the customer, it is backed up by highly trained sales and technical teams. Support packages are all part of the service and the computer is an industry standard requirement.

And, as customers will no doubt find, if they shop with Morelli they will no doubt continue to find that their stock is still at the end of their telephone (fax, modem, web link etc.).

Above left: Slim Moring with one of his cars outside Knebworth House. Above right: One of Morelli's delivery vehicles outside Baird Road premises, Enfield. Below: Neil Laughton of the British Mount Everest Expedition sponsored by the Morelli Group, May 1998.

A partnership that isn't wasting away

When people think of waste their minds turn to time and opportunity. The late Ian Dury even sang about just that in his hit record 'What a Waste'. Push them a little harder and members of the public begin to talk of receptacles under the sink, waste paper bins in the office and tubs in the street for us to dump our fish and chip papers in. Only after some careful thought does the bin man spring to mind. Little do people realise that the content of their wheelie bin is only the tip of the waste processing iceberg. When they are told that LondonWaste Ltd takes in and treats over 1.5 million tonnes of waste annually, it is a figure that is hard to comprehend. However, they do appreciate that it is a lot! Although the collection of waste is a mammoth logistical problem, it is far from the end of the story. Having

collected it, what do you do with it? That seemingly simple question has been vexing environmentalists for years. LondonWaste Ltd does not have all the solutions to the problems on our planet, but it fulfils a major role in dealing with the capital's increasing demands.

The company is the only truly joint venture in the country that combines both the public and private sectors in waste disposal. North LondonWaste Authority is the public face. It came into being after the break up of the former Greater London Council (GLC). The boroughs it serves are Enfield, Barnet, Camden, Waltham Forest, Hackney, Haringey and Islington. The private sector is represented by SITA

Above: *One of the refuse disposal wagons from the 1930s.* ***Below:*** *A view of the premises in the 1950s.*

regard waste as something that has to be disposed of. LondonWaste takes the better view that waste material is a resource. As much waste as possible should be recycled. If it can't be recycled, it should be incinerated so that the electricity and heat generated can be returned to the houses and factories from which the waste came. The Edmonton plant provides enough electricity to power 24,000 homes. Each time you put an empty carton into the bin just think of it as part of the light bulb glowing above your head.

Ever since Southgate Council opened its first incinerating plant at Barrowell Green, Winchmore Hill in 1909, refuse disposal has gradually changed. Before a properly organised system our streets were like open sewers. Litter and rubbish lay where it was dumped to rot away and pass on disease. Council collection, rubbish tips and the burning of waste helped clean up our Victorian towns and cities. But, as the population rocketed, it all had to take place on a much larger scale. At the Southgate Refuse Destructor, as it was known, collecting vans arrived

(GB) Ltd, a subsidiary of Europe's largest waste management company. Together these sectors form LondonWaste Ltd, which employs a workforce of 200 all dedicated to waste disposal, recycling and energy production in the most environmentally friendly manner possible. Households alone produce 800,000 tonnes annually of which 500,000 tonnes is taken to the energy from waste plant at Edmonton. The remainder is collected from hospitals and commercial organisations. The energy from waste plant was called the green power station, a state that became greener in 1996 when a multi million pound investment was made in new equipment and technology. It would be foolish to

Above left: The boiler house and bunkers under construction in February 1969. ***Top:*** The main distribution compound in June 1969.

to tip their loads into chutes that took the rubbish into large trucks. A system of winches took the contents of the trucks to the furnaces where the intense heat reduced the contents to ash. The clinker, or ash, that was left behind usually comprised of nearly a quarter of the weight of waste that had entered the furnace. Even the best part of a century ago it was realised that there could be usefulness from waste. The clinker was recycled in many forms. It made artificial bricks and slabs, sewage filters and was used in mortar making. The Southgate plant was not just a place for rubbish disposal. Its management also had a regard for the welfare of its employees. They were provided with toilets, a bathroom and a cooking range. LondonWaste Ltd has inherited that attitude of consideration towards the people who serve the company.

The first incinerating plant was successful, but the increasing demands of industry and the general public led to the opening of a second one at Barrowell Green. Southgate's population had doubled to 60,000 in the 25 years the plant had been open. By 1935 the new one was ready. A greater use of gas and electricity in cooking meant that a lot of the food going into homes was in cartons and boxes. A greater variety of other material meant that resaleable items, or those that could be reclaimed, were separated out from the rest. The new plant continued in use for the next 30 years and part of the site is still used as a recycling facility.

Further changes in the content and nature of refuse meant alterations in response. As central heating became the norm, less was burned on the household fire. Promotional packaging increased the amount of waste, not to mention its nature.

After the war most of Enfield's waste was collected by the borough and either incinerated at local depots or landfilled within Greater London.

Above left: *Today's hi-tech computer systems.*
Top: *LondonWaste today.*

However, there are no available landfill sites within the city any more. Waste is sent to neighbouring counties for landfill but even there the sites are filling up. Wherever possible, LondonWaste takes the view that recycling and recovery in the form of energy from waste are vital components to its waste management strategy. Even the ash that is produced by incineration is finding its way back into circulation. It is intended that as much as 125,000 tonnes will make its way each year into converted use as road and building materials.

It is now over 30 years since Edmonton Energy From Waste Plant opened. During that period the country has become increasingly aware of the need for an environmentally friendly approach by all of industry. Most have responded well, but not everyone appreciates some of the efforts that have been made. It is all too easy to stand and look at steam drifting from cooling towers and mistakenly make comments about smoke pollution. The reality at the Edmonton plant is that the emissions are continuously monitored and are subject to scrutiny from the Government's Environment Agency. Following a £15 million investment in 1996, the plant is now one of the cleanest plants in Europe. Even the water used in the plant is recycled, having been taken, after treatment, from the local sewerage works. This recycled water has also been used to construct a pond on the LondonWaste site for aquatic plant and animal species. Enhanced habitats encourage a diversity of micro life whilst improving the ecology of the hill within the site and is actually doing something people can appreciate. Tree planting and the provision of birds' nesting boxes are a sign of care within the community.

It was on 15 December 1994 that LondonWaste Ltd became responsible for disposing of the waste from the seven former GLC boroughs that came under the North London Authority. Contracts with rail companies have meant that much of the waste for

landfill is moved out of London, but keeps the problem off the roads. However, extension of the capacity at Edmonton should produce a twofold benefit. Less rubbish will be on the move and a greater amount of electricity will be generated on site. An extra capacity of 150,000 MWh should be possible. That would provide enough power to serve an additional 12,000 homes. The future is both bright and clean.

Above left: *A view of the site today.* ***Above right:*** *An incinerator being inspected by engineers.*
Left: *An aerial view of the Edmonton premises today.*

Delivering the service

As the young driver/gunner steered the military vehicle across the dusty plains of Palestine, little could he realise how this experience with the Royal Artillery would influence and guide the course of his life.

As the driving force behind the continued success of R A Haulage, Reginald Humphry has always been at his best behind a wheel and on being demobbed from the army in 1947, he spent his early civvy years as a driver for various companies.

Delivering for such notables as Sims Bananas and Solo soft drinks, Reg quickly realised that he could offer much more than just a delivery service and laid plans to set out on his own. In 1954, just prior to his marriage to wife Betty, Reg founded the present company, and has been going from strength to strength ever since.

Purchasing a small van, he began by making deliveries for engineering companies in the Finsbury Park area of North London and, before long, had graduated to a larger seven ton flat vehicle.

This investment proved worthwhile as it enabled Reg to seek more ambitious contracts such as delivering building materials for General Asphalt. At this time, Reg was still running a one-man business, though Betty provided much needed administration support to balance up the business.

Although the business was originally based at Kentish Town, two years into the business, Reg considered it better business sense to make a move to Camden Town, where he rented a haulage yard owned by British Rail.

Above left: *Reginald Humphry during his Royal Artillery days.* ***Below:*** *Reg (centre) with friends at Sims Bananas in 1949.*

The move paid off as more lucrative contracts were offered, boosted by Reg's decision to replace his vehicles with 10 ton Bedford flat lorries, complete with railway swop bodies and - eventually replaced by the more spacious 10 ton Luton boxes.

More general haulage work continued, though Reg remained open-minded as to the diversity of delivery work. Jobs ranged from household removals and exhibition work to wagon-loads of banana deliveries from the Royal Albert Dock in East London, not to mention his existing regular workload, delivering for the local printing trade.

In 1965, Reg and Betty bought out a rival haulage company, P Evernden Ltd, which proved particularly worthwhile with extra work involved and proved to be a highly profitable long-term investment as Reg and Betty continue to run it today.

But sixties' London was changing. The gradual demise of the London docks and the advent of containerisation left Reg and Betty forced to seek alternative haulage work, and they made a shift from general haulage work to food and drink distribution.

While this particular grey cloud hung heavy over many haulage companies, it proved to have a silver lining for Reg and Betty. In 1968, they won a contract for major delivery work with grocery giants, H.J.Heinz, and the very next year saw a further move to Ponder's End.

Above: Reg (on the left) in Egypt - 1947.
Right: The firm's first artic pictured here in 1980.

Always providing a reliable service, Reg and Betty were delighted when Heinz offered them more and more work, so much so, that they began to phase out their household removals and exhibition work in the early seventies - with Heinz becoming a major source of work.

This flurry of extra work called for larger, heavier vehicles to be purchased so Reg replaced the old 10 tonners with the more versatile 16 ton lorries, though the existing line of smaller Bedford trucks were still used for smaller, lighter haulage contracts. The company bought its first artic lorry in 1979, clocking - in at a gross vehicle weight of 32 tons. This assured that fewer trips were needed when making multi-drop deliveries to supermarket chains.

continue to provide H J Heinz with a high-quality delivery service - and this has led to becoming a major haulage contractor with other notable companies.

In 1983, Reg and Betty welcomed their eldest son David into the company, followed by his younger brother Philip in 1991. Both are qualified engineers and had gained considerable experience in other areas of the industry, and the couple considered that their sons' wider knowledge and expertise could only add to the existing business opportunities for the company.

This experience stood their sons' and the company's interests in good stead, and they found it enabled them to take over the management of the company, allowing Reg and Betty to take a long-earned rest.

The couple have only taken semi-retirement and, although well over retirement age, they both still take an active interest in the company and continue to work there on a part-time basis.

The year 1985, saw a further move by R A Haulage, as they re-located to a large depot on the Montagu industrial estate in Edmonton - and that same year saw the company diversifying into warehousing. With the offer of major distribution work for Nestle, the future of the company seemed assured, so they invested in the purchase of a whole fleet of Volvo trucks.

Today, the majority of the vehicles used by the company are 38/41 tonne artics with tri-axle curtain-sided and box trailers; and the fleet of 14 vehicles consist of a mixture of tractor units and rigids. This wide range of transport has led R A Haulage to

Nestle is a major source of work for R A Haulage and they are also proud to have been associated with H J Heinz for so many years; they are one of the longest serving hauliers for that company.

Reg and Betty Humphry have come a long way since Reg bought a small van to make deliveries for engineering companies in Finsbury Park.

And what of his success? Reg Humphry still maintains that the first rule of any business is to provide a first-class service. He says that the buying power of the main supermarket chains has resulted in major changes in distribution share. National companies may continue to win major contracts, but the principle remains the same for any haulage company, big or small.

Even smaller companies, such as R A Haulage, must concentrate on providing a first-class service to smaller manufacturers and retailers. Satisfied customers, who come back for more, are the best advertisements a company can offer.

And, if anything, the success of R A Haulage stands as a testament to that.

Top left: *Some of the vehicles from 1985.*
Top right: *Reg in 1980.* **Above left:** *Part of the modern fleet.* **Below:** *Reg in May 2000.*

Sauces for courses

There can be few if any readers who have not enjoyed the delicious taste of a vanilla flavoured ice cream - but how many of us know what vanilla is?

Natural vanilla is derived from the dark aromatic beans which are the only true source of the luxurious vanilla flavour.

Vanilla beans are the product of a dramatically flowering relative of the orchid. They first arrived in Europe in the 16th century and are now principally cultivated on islands off the east coast of Africa. One, the island of Madagascar, produces 50 per cent of the world's natural vanilla. The annual world crop of vanilla beans amounts to just 1,500 tonnes which almost entirely becomes essence for use in ice-cream, confectionery, bakery products and soft drinks.

But what is the connection between Madagascar and Enfield?

The answer can be found at Rayner & Co Ltd in Bull Lane, a firm founded in 1851 by John Rayner, a pharmacist in Kent, for the manufacture of flavouring, essences and medicines. By the 1880s the business had relocated to Clerkenwell Road. By 1911

Above: A very up-market advertisement for Burgess' range of Anchovy products. Below: The Bottling Room in the 1950s

however the firm had fallen on hard times and was only rescued from bankruptcy by two brothers L H Stockwell and A J Stockwell who joined the firm in 1912.

Under its new proprietors the factory was moved to Holloway from where it operated until 1930 when the Edmonton factory was built.

In 1954 Rayner & Co Ltd acquired the even older business of John Burgess & Son Ltd. John Burgess had started his business in 1760 selling Epicurean imports - high quality luxury foods - to the nobility and gentry. Lord Nelson took several Burgess delicacies with him to the Battle of the Nile. Burgess products were soon deemed essential rations by globe-trotting Englishmen building the British Empire and a prestigious Royal Warrant was awarded in 1853 by Queen Victoria, a warrant which is still proudly held to this day. Burgess delicacies were even amongst the rations hauled on sledges by Captain Scott's Antarctic expedition in 1910. The tradition continues to this day: Rayner Burgess supplied the 'In the Footsteps of Scott Antarctic expedition in 1984-86' and supplied relishes to Operation Raleigh.

In the same year, 1954, that Rayners bought John Burgess and Son it also acquired the well known 'Crusha' brand of Milk Shake Syrups, an item which today is the company's largest single product line.

During the decade of the fifties other flavour companies were acquired too, including Supreme, A B Marshal and Goodwin Tidswell & Co - collectively forming the Rayner Essence Group Ltd.

The new group's strengths included an unrivalled expertise in the development of flavours for ice-cream production including a wide range of vanilla essences and experience in flavours, essences and colours for baking, confectionery food products and soft drinks. In addition to flavours and colours Rayner's became major suppliers of syrups for milkshakes, ice cream and dairy toppings, ripples and soft drinks and cordials. The firm imported its own vanilla beans to be processed into natural vanilla essences which could then be provided to customers either pure or fortified as they are required.

By the end of the 20th century a computer system would be giving instant recall of thousands of recipes dating from 1851 to the present.

Right: Rayner's Salad Cream in the 1950s.
Above: Cocktail cherries, the very epitome of 1960s style. Top: The present-day state of the art factory at Rayner's.

A highly experienced research team would use the new technology to the full to produce new flavours to match individual customers needs.

In 1986 the Edmonton factory was expanded and completely modernised with prestigious new offices and laboratories provided to allow for further expansion in the 1990s.

In the 1980s Rayner & Co Ltd decided to widen its product range into the health food sector. In 1987 the firm acquired Cauldron Foods, a tofu manufacturing company which was then based in Bristol but which has since moved to Portishead.

In 1990 the business became part of the Hero Group, a Swiss-based European food company, though Rayner's continued to supply its own range of products plus a range of Hero branded items to both the retail and catering trades.

Seven years later in 1997, backed by Royal Bank Development Capital Ltd - part of the Royal Bank of Scotland, Rayner's recovered its independence following a management buy-out from the Hero group.

As a result of the buy-out Rayner & Co Ltd formed the Rayner Food Group Ltd comprising Rayner & Co, Rayner Essence, Rayner Burgess and

Cauldron Foods. Just three years later, in 2000, the new group was able to expand by acquiring Martlet Natural Foods and West Country Honey Farms.

Today the company is a £32 million pound business specialising in the manufacture of sauces, condiments, flavouring, essences and health foods, the latter being significantly added to by the acquisition of Martlet Natural foods in Wellingborough Northamptonshire. Martlet's manufactures several well known products not least PLJ pure lemon juice as well as a variety of vinegars, conserves, chutneys and honeys.

The acquisition of Martlet diversified Rayner's product portfolio and significantly increased the size of its manufacturing and technical capabilities. Rayner's Managing Director Geoff Kirby comments 'Since the management buy-out from Hero in 1997 our strategic plan has been to grow the business both organically and through acquisitions. Martlet had a number of synergies with our business and provided us with an immediate and complementary product portfolio. Martlet's expert knowledge and technical ability in the development of organic products provided an ideal platform for us to develop and capitalise on that fast-growing sector of the food industry'.

Rayner & Co Ltd has retained its base at Edmonton which together with its health food production at Portishead and Martlet Foods at Northampton comprises a work force approaching 300. The company is one of the largest suppliers of private label condiments to the grocery industry. In addition the company boasts a number of branded product lines including Burgess Condiments (which carry the Royal Warrant) Burgess Speciality Sauces, Rayner Essences and Flavourings and Crusha Milk Shake Syrups.

The ingredients for products bearing the Rayner name have in many instances arrived in Edmonton from the far flung corners of the globe, and after being processed they are frequently re-exported back to exotic places. One cannot help but wonder if long-haul visitors to the island of Madagascar enjoying a vanilla flavoured ice cream whilst shaded from the tropical sun by palm trees will ever reflect that one element of their cooling snack may have already made the same journey as them - and back again!

Left: *An early advert for Burgess' Tartare Sauce.*
Above left: *A 1960s advert for Crusha Milkshake.*

Two test tube babies

Who first discovered glass? Some say it was the ancient Phoenicians. One thing is sure: the art or craft of making and blowing glass was developed far back in the history of mankind. At a time when mass production is the norm and craft skills are often replaced by machinery there remains a demand for specialist glass products for use in laboratories everywhere. Even those of us who have never stepped foot in a commercial laboratory will be familiar with scientific glassware from our schooldays or from laboratories depicted in television and cinema where glass retorts and test tubes abound. But where does all that equipment come from? One answer is Enfield, and two firms in particular: G Farley and Aimer Products.

George Farley, the founder of G Farley & Sons Ltd, started his working life as a glassblower for Ediswan the radio valve manufacturers. At the close of the first world war in 1918 George left Ediswan to start his own small business, G Farley & Sons, in an upstairs room in the same building as Russel the Printers in Enfield. The new firm soon moved on to Ponders End High Street, setting up a workshop at the rear of the then Ponders End Post Office.

Working hard to establish his business George Farley was soon doing a great deal of specialised work for the Government and the lighting industry. Following George's

retirement in 1968 the running of the business was left to his grandson Bert Farley.

Bert Farley made a great success of G Farley & Sons Ltd and did a considerable amount of work for the Government Chemist and for large pharmaceutical companies. The company continued to produce specialised glassware for research and also stocked laboratory equipment enabling the firm to supply a large range of such equipment and offer technical expertise in its use.

In 1981 Bert retired and the business was sold to another established glassblowing company, Aimer Products, though kept running as an independent company.

Right: *Atomic symbol made in glass.* **Below:** *Quality Control, testing glassware for use in the laboratory.*

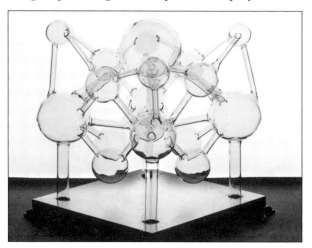

As their knowledge of glassblowing and their business acumen developed the Aimer brothers progressed to the manufacture of all kinds of glassware, including laboratory and scientific glassware.

At the close of the second world war in 1945 the last surviving Aimer brother retired from the business which was then taken over by a two man partnership.

The partnership of Messrs W F Dowden and Doug Sanderson continued to develop Aimer Products for the next thirty years, until 1975, when W F Dowden retired; a few years later Doug Sanderson passed away.

On Doug Sanderson's death the company was then taken over by David Leveridge who had worked for Aimer products for many years; it was he who in 1981 would buy G Farley & Sons and move both companies to their present premises in Brimsdown.

The skills involved in working with glass, first developed in classical times, have been handed down from craftsman to craftsman now for a hundred generations or more. Pioneers such as George Farley and the Aimer brothers continued that tradition during the last century, in the process adding to and improving their knowledge base in a constantly developing industry. That professional baton of the glassblowers craft continues to be passed on. Today the company is a family run business involving David Leveridge's wife, son and daughter.

Following the acquisition by Aimer the firm was moved to Brimsdown where the company is still going strong today, both companies sharing premises in Stockingswater Lane.

The origins of Aimer Products Ltd can be traced back even further than G Farley & Sons, to 1900. In that final year of the 19th century two brothers of the Aimer family decided to enter the field of specialist glassblowing. A company was formed under the name of G C Aimer & Co and the new business began manufacturing in premises located in the Tottenham area of London.

It is of tremendous interest to record the fact that some of the earliest work of these two pioneering brothers was the development and manufacture of x-ray tubes. Specimens of those early tubes may be seen today in the Science Museum at South Kensington in London.

*Top: Glassblower sealing disc into a glass tube for filtering. **Above left:** Glass worked by hand on bench lamp.*

An independent firm enjoying material advantages

Enfield's remaining Independent Builders' Merchant started operations in Southbury Road in 1935, when Long & Somerville opened a small depot at Enfield's derelict Churchbury Station, now known as Southbury Station. However, the site then bore little resemblance to the extensive modern facilities we know today, where modern computer systems provide instant access to the many thousands of lines of stock which are always available.

The business was founded by Mr John Somerville, an ambitious young man who spent the first few years of his working life in the employment of a London timber merchant, and Mr Long, one of the partners in the Liverpool timber merchants Long & Browning. The two men set up an office in East London; they had no warehouse and held no stock, but obtained and delivered building materials to order. Before long, however, the original business strategy was modified. It was recognised that Mr Long, being based in Liverpool, was not in a position to contribute much to the venture, so he withdrew from the partnership. Mr Somerville realised that his best chance of success lay in building up his customer base and holding stock in his own depot. This he did, opening a depot in the Goods Yard at Snaresbrook Station, Wanstead. Shortly afterwards, with the house building industry enjoying something of a boom, he opened a second depot in Enfield, followed by a third in Coventry. By this time Long & Somerville had been incorporated as a Limited Company, with Mr Len Griggs as a Director.

During the war the company was on call seven days a week for blitz damaged buildings

Below: *The original premises at Snarebrook Station, Wanstead.*

The outbreak of the second world war compelled Mr Somerville to alter his business plans yet again. The activities of the building trade and the distribution of building materials came under strict government control. Repairs to houses, shops and factories which had been damaged in the blitz were a priority, and Long & Somerville Ltd was on call seven days a week to supply materials for this purpose. Both Enfield and Coventry suffered in the bombing.

In the aftermath of the war, shortages and restrictions continued to affect trading conditions for many years, but gradually the company was able to start expanding again. One completely new area of growth was the DIY trade. The post-war newly-weds became the first generation of DIY-ers, inspired perhaps by the make-do-and-mend philosophy instilled into them during the war years, and taking advantage of the availability of new man-made materials and products. Long & Somerville increased their range of stock to meet the demands of this new market sector. The firm, headed by Stuart Somerville after his father's retirement, was now serving small and medium-sized builders as well as members of the public. To meet growing demand a new warehouse was built on the Enfield site in 1968. Eventually it was necessary to acquire more land and construct new offices and trade counter facilities. This was completed in 1982, shortly before the company celebrated its 50th anniversary.

Subsequent decades were to bring a number of challenges in the form of economic recessions and the growth of superstore chains, but Long & Somerville kept the emphasis firmly on quality combined with expert, personal service. Customers are drawn from a radius of approximately ten miles of Southbury Road, from London to Hertford. They include local builders, national building

This page: Long & Somerville today.

contractors, DIY enthusiasts, landscape gardeners, drainage and groundwork contractors. In recent years the company has focused on the heavy side of the industry, specialising in drainage and groundwork items. It holds extensive stocks of bricks, blocks, plaster, plasterboard, aggregates, concrete goods, lintels, roofing materials, drainage and groundwork products together with an excellent range of appropriate hand tools.

But Long & Somerville does more than simply sell builders' materials; it provides a valuable service to the building industry. The company's knowledge and experience means that they understand their customers' requirements. The extensive range of goods is complemented by an efficient delivery service, and backed by expert product knowledge. The staff are able to cope with even the most unusual requests from their customers. 'If the product is made for the building industry, we can usually obtain it,' says Stuart Somerville, current managing director of the company and a former chairman of the London Area of the Builders Merchants Federation.

Since 1935 Long & Somerville's site in Southbury Road has supplied the materials which have enabled the successful completion of countless building projects, large and small. This independent builders' merchant has become an established and respected part of the local building scene - a position which it intends to occupy for many years to come.

Turning up trumps

Walk through the doors at Turnomatic Limited at Edmonton's Angel Road Works and you will notice that the place is a hive of activity. Today this forward thinking company employs 37 people and has recently expanded its floor area with the long term aim of growing the business even further. This well known local business manufactures components for various sectors including the motor and electrical industries and production runs of millions is not uncommon; but where did the company come from?

Back in 1957 the assets of a very small, turned parts manufacturing business were purchased from the owners on their retirement. The company was renamed Turnomatic Ltd and began to specialise in the production of brass components, principally screws, pins and nuts.

Back then the business occupied an old timber structure, a leasehold property just off the High Road, East Finchley. Despite being lethal from the fire risk point of view, with years of cutting oil having been absorbed into the wooden fabric of the premises, it was an ideal building from the point of view of deadening the enormous amount of noise that was generated by the sliding-head automatic lathes which formed the majority of the plant.

> *In 1957 the business occupied an old timber structure, an ideal building for deadening the noise of the machinery*

The lease on the East Finchley premises ran out in 1968 but it was not possible to find another suitable property in the area, so the company was relocated to Cricklewood adjacent to the major electrical wiring accessory manufacturer Contactum Ltd, an existing customer that was expanding rapidly at that time. By giving Turnomatic the lion's share of its orders for turned parts, Contactum played a major role in the development of the company which was becoming a specialist in manufacturing for the electrical wiring accessory field, subsequently supplying over the following years leading companies like Volex, Lewden, MK, Home Automation, Timeguard, Tadmod, Marbo and G E Alsthom.

Below: *Ron Hunt at work in Unit 8, Edmonton, December 1994.*

with a change of management and Turnomatic was very fortunate to be able to persuade Bob Fenwick to run the company as General Manager; he had a wealth of experience and contacts in the turned parts industry and was able to diversify the company's activities into supplying many different types of component to a whole new range of customers.

Bob Fenwick further developed the use of rotary transfer machines which were ideal for short and medium volume production runs, but by now Turnomatic was also becoming involved in very high volume production. Bob purchased twelve 'Eubama' machines which proved to be ideal for the purpose; those high volume machines enabled Turnomatic to continue to flourish in a highly competitive market.

Why has the company continued to thrive? According to Bob Fenwick, one of their strengths is that the company is able to offer its customers consistency of supply. For example they work a 'just in time' practice with a customer in Liverpool helping them to effectively control their stock and maintain their customers' production.

To meet the increasing demand for its components for electrical accessories the company could no longer rely on its automatic lathes alone and, after the move to Cricklewood, developed an expertise in rotary transfer machines, purchasing many of the extremely adaptable 'Vertomat' machines during the 1970s and 1980s. The Vertomat machines were originally designed for fast production of small machined components from bar or hand-loaded blanks and with the addition of new equipment became extremely versatile. By 1988 Turnomatic had outgrown the property in Cricklewood but once again was unable to find a suitable property in the immediate vicinity. Fortunately an ideal property was located, much closer to the original Turnomatic site, this time at the Angel Road Works in Edmonton. The move to the present site coincided

Today the equipment used at Turnomatic is very sophisticated and operators learn feeding, operating and toolsetting skills along with manufacturing knowledge. Many skills are transferable but at the same time highly specialised. As the company has grown new sectors of work have been researched but new work has meant a shortage of skilled labour. To maintain a measured growth Bob Fenwick intends to set up a training programme for new recruits helping people leaving school to learn skills and at the same time pass on the traditions which have now served Turnomatic well during six decades.

Top: *The small tool room in Unit 8.*
Above left: *Exhibiting in the Jobscene exhibition at Alexandra Palace in November 1997.*

A focal point for town centre shopping

When people say that they are off to the Palace Gardens, do not think that they have regal ideas above their station. It is not Buckingham Palace to which they are referring, but the focal point of retailing facilities in Enfield - the Palace Gardens Shopping Centre. The complex manager might say that they were on the right track with their statement. After all, it is a right royal shopping experience! The days are long gone when shoppers had to trudge along the streets, lashed by rain and blown about by the autumnal winds. For the Enfield housewife there is no more tramping along the slushy January pavements to get a bargain in the sales. All she needs is now under one roof. In the Centre she can find three large stores and 37 other shops. The complex is arranged around a pedestrianised area that links Church Street with Sydney Road. Much of the mall has a canopy roof that protects shoppers from the unpredictable British weather. But, it is not just a shopping centre. It has a warm and welcoming feel to it. Large enough to cater for everything from the weekly groceries to the latest pop CDs,

the Centre is still compact enough to make people feel comfortable. Some of the massive out of town malls that have sprung up in recent years across the country are so big that they become impersonal and lack a sense of identity. They have no soul. Not only that, but it is easy to lose your sense of direction and get completely lost. Heaven help you if you have not made a careful note of where your car was parked or you could be searching forever! The Palace Gardens, happily, has been able to keep its individuality whilst fulfilling a valuable community service.

The Centre was built by McAlpine and opened in 1982. Its concrete frame and reinforced brick elevations, under a part mansard tiled roof, lend an air of distinction to Enfield's retail centre. The site has had a distinguished past. It was once part of the Crown's lands. A manor house that stood here dates back over 600 years. As it was known as Enfield Palace, then the royal reference to shopping here is not many a mile from the mark!

Both pictures: *The centre of Enfield in the early days of the 20th century. The Cedar tree can be seen behind the buildings in the picture below.*

major attention of tree preservation orders. The manor house went with it and a direct link with our past disappeared as well. At least the name of the shopping centre has kept an indirect connection, for it was built in the grounds of the old Enfield Palace. The Centre's logo has also kept the tree and gardens alive in people's memories. Pearson's Department Store now covers the site of the actual manor house.

Now that we have given some thought to the history of the Palace Gardens Shopping Centre, perhaps that first

When the connection with the Royal Family was lost, the house changed hands on a number of occasions. At one time it was a private school. The famous Dr Robert Uvedale founded the school in the 17th century. His reputation as a botanist was world wide. Dr Uvedale collected rare and exotic species of plants from across the globe. One of his most memorable imports was the cedar tree. He was among the first to bring this now familiar tree to Britain. The cedar that he planted showed its durability. it stood from 1663 until it was chopped down in 1927. That was in the days before 'Woodman, woodman - spare that tree' or the

notion about the elevated status of its shoppers was not too far off beam, after all. There is certainly a nobility about shopping here that ranks the Palace Gardens as a cut above its rivals. Maybe, some of that historical tradition has rubbed off on both the management and its customers. It is a special place to be and retailers have a sense of importance and purpose in providing a service that makes the humblest shopper feel like royalty.

*Above: Work well under way on the new Palace Gardens development, 1982. **Top:** A busy high street scene from the early 1970s.*

Yoplait Dairy Crest - La crème de la crème

R aines Dairy Foods was an established family business based in Enfield, which was sold to Yoplait Dairy Crest (YDC) in 1998. The amalgamation made the business into one of the largest producers of fresh dairy products in the country. The venture meant that there was now a wide range of branded products available in addition to the 'Supermarket own label' and ingredient dairy products established by Raines. The more adventurous palates of 21st century Britons have taken to the style of yogurt, soft cheese, cream, buttermilk and smatana. Tasty dips before dinner parties and delicious children's desserts at tea time are catered for by YDC.

If inventive names such as Petits Filous, Frubes, Wildlife and Yop conjure up a mixture of the exotic and the tasty, both would be true. The continental attraction of the products is not a surprise. Yoplait is

Above centre: Two advertisements for the company's produce from the early 1980s.
Right: *Original Raines products under the Yoplait brand name.*

part of France's largest milk co-operative that had become established in Britain in the 1980s. As Britons travel more and widen the scope of their own larders it is just as common to hear the words fromage frais as bangers and mash. Although the head office is in Crown Road, there are other centres across the South of England. Whilst Enfield produces yogurts, soft cheese and cream (much of which is sold in large containers to be used as ingredients by other manufacturers), Basildon produces retail yogurts. To the west, Yeovil manufactures ice cream and chilled desserts.

Raines Dairy Foods was founded in 1910 by Lewis Raine. He was a horse trader who hitched his horses to carts to deliver the first soft cooking cheese Raines Dairy Foods ever produced. Lewis built up a clientele in the East End of London amongst the Jewish community. Many of them were immigrants from Poland. They took well to the 'Curd Cheese' he supplied. Bakeries in the Petticoat Lane area became major customers

Raines Dairy Foods Ltd

NOT ONLY –
are we the leading private company packaging "own brand" fresh dairy products for the major multiples

BUT ALSO –
we offer a full range of pre-pack and bulk YOGURTS – MR MEN YOGURTS – COTTAGE CHEESES – SOFT CHEESES and CREAM to Independant Supermarkets – Delicatessens – Caterers – Hoteliers and Food Manufacturers.

IF YOU WANT THE BEST QUALITY & SERVICE CONTACT US!

Raines Dairy Foods Ltd **R**

NOT ONLY – are we the leading private company packaging "own brand" fresh dairy products for the major multiples

BUT ALSO – we offer a full range of pre-pack and bulk YOGURTS – MR MEN YOGURTS – COTTAGE CHEESES – SOFT CHEESES and CREAM to Independant Supermarkets – Delicattessens – Caterers – Hoteliers and Food Manufacturers.

IF YOU WANT THE BEST QUALITY & SERVICE CONTACT US!

| Head Office: London Area Depot 15-21 Northwold Road London N16 7HP 01-249 1551 | Midlands Depot: Walker Industrial Est. Station Road, Coleshill Birmingham B46 3LN 0675-63494 | Northern Depot: 7 Stanley Street Manchester M8 8GQ 061-834 2562 | Western Depots: Grove Road Wantage Oxon 02357-66221 | Hercules Way Bowerhill Melksham 0225 704785 |

horse, either. Always one to seek profit from a crisis, he asked her out for a meal as some form of recompense. When the shop assistant calmed down enough to listen, she accepted. They married before the year was out!

The story goes to show the flexibility that was Mr Raine and is still part of the ethic of YDC. Providing a quality service has always been the aim. A third generation of Raines took the reins in the early 1990s when Nigel Raine became managing director on the death of his father. He continued to direct the company growth in supplying its products to all the major supermarket giants in addition to the traditional smaller and specialist retail outlets. Nigel had nearly 30 years learning the ropes from his father and was the company's production director before assuming control. He retired when the company was sold to YDC.

From small beginnings, the company has come a long way. The increased investment planned by YDC for the 21st century can only see it go even further.

and the company expanded and began manufacturing in Stoke Newington. By coincidence, the bakery connection was re-established in 1976. The old premises were unsuitable for redevelopment to meet the company's further expansion plans. The factory site that was purchased in Enfield had once been a bakery. Raines moved its offices to the new site alongside the factory in 1985.

Lewis Raine was joined in the business by his son, Mr I Raine. He began by helping deliver the dairy products from his horse and cart. Horses are nicer creatures than noisy vans, but they do have habit of getting you into trouble. Whilst making a delivery to one shop the young Mr Raine returned to his cart, only to find that the horse had started to devour a display of straw hats outside the neighbouring shop. Before he could sneak away with his reputation intact, he was confronted by an irate young shop assistant. She gave him the dressing down of a lifetime. She was none too complimentary to the

*Above: Stills from a recent advertising campaign for Petits Filous. **Right:** One of the delivery lorries outside the premises.*

Good things in store

Twenty-first century Enfield is accustomed to relying on Pearson's for all manner of things, from furniture to fashion accessories - even a new hair-do. A century ago, however, the business was simply a draper's. Brothers Stanley and Arthur Pearson started out by purchasing an existing drapery business in Enfield, where they employed four sales ladies, two salesmen and a porter whose duties included delivering goods by bicycle, and soon began to prosper.

A few years later they acquired a second shop, and opened more departments. Expansion was then halted by the war, but afterwards, during the 1920s and 1930s, the brothers bought a number of properties in the centre of Enfield, including the old Elizabethan Palace. In 1921 the present building opened its doors to customers, and the premises were enlarged in 1931 and again in 1936. By this time, departments included a furniture showroom, run by Sydney Pearson, the younger brother of Stanley and Arthur.

Stanley Pearson retired in 1941, and the business became a private limited company, with Arthur as Governing Director. After the war his son Jack was appointed to the board, and took over as Managing Director in 1965. By this time Pearson's was beginning to bear more resemblance to the store which we know today. The first floor extension was built in the mid 1950s, followed by another large extension in 1962. Substantial alterations were made to the rear of the premises around the same time, resulting in a number of new departments and services including a restaurant and a ladies' hairdressing salon. However, further major developments still lay ahead, and many readers will remember the opening of the three-storey extension in 1982, following the completion of the Palace Gardens Shopping Precinct. This brought us a new sports department on the ground floor and new carpet and furniture departments on the first and second floors, with a passenger lift. More recently still, in 1988, a bedding department was opened in newly-acquired premises on London Road.

Throughout the 20th century Pearson's has continued to grow, bringing its customers an increasingly wide range of quality goods and services. Its staff has grown to around 300, and branches have been opened in Bishop's Stortford, Loughton and Wood Green. Headed by Mrs Marjorie Pearson, widow of Jack Pearson, who took over as Chairman after the death of her husband in 1994, the family business is now approaching its centenary. Pearson's is an established part of life in Enfield, and we trust it will remain so for many, many years to come.

Below: *The premises pictured in the early 1900s.*

Enfield's favourite shoe repairer

It was a sad day for Enfield when George and Gwen Fullick locked the door of their Lincoln Road shoe repair business for the last time. George Fullick had started the business in 1953 after completing a government training course in shoe repairing. At this time no less than 23 other shoe repairers competed for trade in the district. All kinds of work was undertaken, from routine shoe repairs to surgical work and repairs to belts, leather coats, golf bags and even tents! The business was first established in small shop premises located at Harman Road, Bush Hill Park, Enfield. By 1954 George had courted and married Gwen, the love of his life. The couple were blessed with the birth of a daughter, Linda, in 1955. Linda grew up to be an experienced and knowledgeable reference librarian in North London, much to the delight of her proud parents.

Older residents may remember the couple as 'the Raylicks' - a consequence of a short-lived partnership with a Mr Rayner which resulted in the business being called *Raylick Shoe Service*. The name stuck though the partnership didn't, and Mr and Mrs Fullick saw no reason to alter their trading style during the 35 years they were in business.

George Fullick is modest about his achievements as a businessman and an accomplished cyclist. In his youth, as member of the *Priory Wheelers Cycling Club,* he rode the 241 miles from Barnet to Sutton on Trent and back in less than 13 hours. Journeys of up to 14 mile per day to work and back were carried out for years on end as a matter of routine. George attributes much of his business success to his wife Gwen who, he says, was astute with money, supportive in business with the rare ability to charm and delight customers.

Continued success led to a move to Lincoln Road, Bush Hill Park in 1968 into larger freehold premises. The *Fullicks* were to enjoy a further happy 20 years at this location, living in the maisonette above the shop and relaxing in the well-kept garden at the rear of the property when time permitted.

When George and Gwen retired in 1988 the number of shoe repairers in the district had fallen to just four, including a small heel bar. Looking back over the years they were in business George and Gwen Fullick speak proudly of the service they provided for generations of delighted customers and the large number of friends they made over the counter of their busy shop.

Top: *George Fullick hard at work behind the counter of his first shop located at Harman Road. The photograph dates from 1954.*

Left: *The Priory Wheelers Club Dinner in January 1954 at Firs Hall, Enfield. The event saw George Fullick receive an award from Eileen Sheridan, herself an accomplished time trialist.*

The open air swimming baths that graced the corner of Great Cambridge Road and Southbury Road in a picture dating from the summer of 1932

Acknowledgments

Many local people and organisations have provided invaluable assistance and permission to reproduce precious photographs to enable us to publish this book and we are delighted to acknowledge their help here: Camera Craft Ltd; Graham Dalling, Local History Officer, and Enfield Leisure Services; George and Gwen Fullick; Eileen Goostree; Peter Hodge and Southgate Civic Trust; Janet Lane; Bren Neal; Harold Neville; Sheila Nielsen; Kenneth Prater; Doreen Rost; Stephen Sellick; Peter G. Wells.

*Thanks are also due to
Andrew Mitchell who penned the editorial text
and Steve Ainsworth and Margaret Wakefield for their copywriting skills*